El Discreto

ISBN 978-1-945028-52-6

First published by St. Vitus Dance

Book design and production assistance by Adam Robinson for
Good Book Developers (goodbookdevelopers.com)

Cover art by Freddy Guerrero
@ @tattoosbyfreddy

Please visit https://StVitus.Dance

"We become like that which we love. If we love what is vile, we become vile; but if we love what is virtuous, we become virtuous."

—Father Fulton Sheen

El Discreto

The Complete Man (1646)

Baltasar Gracián

Translated by M. San Pedro

CONTENTS

Preliminary Note

I, M. San Pedro, present a modernized English translation of *El Discreto (1646)* by Lorenzo Gracián[1] of Huesca, Spain, based on the Spanish edition from Manuel Arroyo Stephens titled *Obras completas de Baltasar Gracián*, Madrid, Tuner Libros, 1993, vol. II. In order to facilitate the reading of the text for the non-specialized public, I chose to offer a modernized edition allowing for further clarification of Gracián's *conceptismo* style of writing and, when I considered it appropriate, issued amendments to the text in order to make it easier to comprehend in contemporary times. These amendments are few and seldom, only occurring where I felt that further clarification was needed for the benefit of the reader. It was of the utmost importance to me that I present a version that preserves the integrity of the original writing, even in its punctuation and spacing. I am more than certain that this modern English translation will be found insightful, lucid, digestible, and, most importantly, effective.

---

1   Lorenzo Gracián is the pseudonym under which Baltasar Gracián first began publishing. Only his closest friends, Dr. Juan Francisco Andrés, Don Vincencio Juan de Lastanosa, Dr. Juan Orencio de Lastanosa, and Dr. Don Manuel de Salinas y Lizana, knew of his real identity.

About this Book

El Discreto: The Complete Man (1646) is a practical manual by Baltasar Gracián, belonging to the genre of didactic prose and intended to teach, particularly through moral instruction as an ulterior motive. It describes how an intelligent and discreet man must behave, not just in seventeenth-century Spain but also in the modern world. With this treatise, Gracián continues in the line of his previous works dedicated to moral philosophy. It is divided into twenty-five chapters that describe the virtues that are needed to enhance wisdom, elegance, culture, good education, and proper behavior in the Complete Man. This book by Gracián proposes, among other requirements to achieve full discretion, to always exercise genius and ingenuity, to be a man of consistency, and to refrain from the use of indecent humor. Culture and refinement, intellect and discernment, gallantry, and observation are essential qualities for every man who desires to be a Complete Man.

This book also presents important divergences from his previous works. For example, the protagonist is no longer an exceptional man, as portrayed in his book, *El Héroe: The Hero (1637)*. Now he is a prudent man who needs many qualities to develop himself in society. And unlike the hero, who aspired to be the formation of the perfect statesman, Gracián explains in parts, the singular and eminent aspects that are representative of the Complete Man when he knows how to realize himself in society.

Preface

Baltasar Gracián was born in Belmonte de Calatayud, which has since been renamed Belmonte de Gracián, in the province of Zaragoza, in the Kingdom of Aragon, on January 8, 1601. This year, 2023, marks the 422nd anniversary of his birth. In 1619, at the age of 18, he entered the Jesuit Order in Tarragona, of which he remained a member until the end of his life, on December 6, 1658.

The different positions he held—Chair of Philosophy at the University of Gandía, preacher and confessor in Huesca, confessor to the Viceroy of Aragón, vice-rector in Tarragona, preacher and professor of Scripture in Zaragoza—allowed him to come into contact with some of the best scholars and intellectuals of his time and gave him access to some of the largest libraries in Spain, such as that of Spanish Noble and Knight, Don Vincencio Juan de Lastanosa in Huesca, Spain, which contained more than 7000 volumes. Don Lastanosa would go on to significantly impact Gracián's future by becoming his patron and by encouraging him to publish his first and second treatises: *El Héroe (1637)*, a critique of Niccolo Machiavelli and a discourse on Christian leadership, and *El Politico (1640)*, a treatise on the ideal image of a politician, fashioned after and in homage to, the diplomatic mastery of King Fernando II of Aragon, the Great Catholic King.

Historically, Gracián is considered the most representative writer of the Spanish literary style known as *Conceptismo (Conceptism)* and its leading exponent. A style of writing

that began during the Spanish Golden Age, it is charac-
terized by its rapid rhythm, directness, simple vocabulary,
witty metaphors, and wordplay; multiple meanings are con-
veyed in a very concise manner, and conceptual intricacies
are emphasized over elaborate vocabulary; it is a style that is
very distinguishable and very present throughout this book.

During his lifetime, some of his works were translated into
French and distributed in Spanish in Portugal; in the kingdoms of Spain, however, he faced harsh criticism. In the
18th century, some of his works were translated into German,
Dutch, Polish, Romanian, Hungarian, and Russian.

But he was only rediscovered and labeled as a significant and
eminent author towards the end of the 19th and the beginning of the 20th century, by German philosophers Arthur
Schopenhauer and Friedrich Nietzsche. In Spain, he did not
attain equal consideration until the beginning of the 20th
century, at the same time Góngora's sonnet *"El Greco"* was
rediscovered.

Since then, Gracián has become a well-known and preeminent author. Two of his books have become especially
famous: *El Oráculo Manual y Arte de Prudencia (1647)*,
translated most famously in 1992 as *The Art of Worldly
Wisdom* by Professor Christopher Maurer, and *El Criticón
(1651-1657)*, translated as *The Critic* by Sir Paul Rycaut
in 1681. But the catalog of writings belonging to this wise
Aragonese, who considered himself more a writer than a
man of piety, did not stop at these two titles. Gracián wrote
a total of nineteen books, seven of which were published.
The other twelve were unfortunately burned as a form of
censorship during his persecution for repeatedly publishing
works that his superiors did not approve.

All those that were published are equally superb treatises, including what is perhaps his best yet most unknown work, the one you are currently reading: *El Discreto: The Complete Man (1646)*.

At a moment in history when Western civilization is in rapid decline due to apostasy and the loss of the traditional family structure and all it upholds; where masculinity is under constant attack in both our media and culture by malevolent spirits and their insidious hatred for all that is Godly, orderly, and true; and in a society where males make up 70% of all suicides, what it means to be a complete man needs to be correctly defined. As such, this guidebook could not be more timely.

This English translation of *El Discreto* aims to rescue it from the linguistic barrier to which it has been chained for centuries. With it, the mastery and wisdom of this sagacious Catholic Jesuit, whom many consider to be the finest Spanish mind to ever exist, can pierce the darkness surrounding our civilization with its truths, centuries after its inception.

As for me, it has taken almost two years to translate this treatise on manliness and masculinity. The greatest difficulties of this translation were in preserving the integrity of Gracián's writing style and antiquated tone, translating his allegories and parables so that they made perfect sense in English, interpreting his literary style of *conceptismo* and its metaphors, and ensuring that the cleverness of his intellectual acuity and shrewd insight on humanity did not get lost in translation. Moreover, I wanted to personalize the author so that readers feel as if the wise Aragonese were speaking to them directly, instructing them on matters of piety, refinement, rectitude, masculinity and giving them direction in life.

I am intimately familiar with Gracián, his writings, and with this treatise in particular, being its translator. Of all his works, I consider this one to be his greatest and most important: because you can be neither *El Héroe (The Hero)* nor *El Político (The Politician)*, nor understand *El Arte de Ingenio (The Art of Ingenuity)*, unless you are first and foremost *El Discreto: The Complete Man*.

The matter contained in this book, the privilege of translating it, and the friendship that I have established with the spirit of this great Catholic Jesuit have been the most impactful occurrences of my life. It has been my greatest honor to translate this treatise, and I look forward to experiencing the same honor when I translate *El Político (1640)*, *El Arte de Ingenio (1642)*, and *El Comulgatorio (1655)*.

—M. San Pedro

Epigram

From Dr. Juan Francisco Andrés
to Don Vincencio Juan de Lastanosa[2]

How much does all of Spain owe to your genius
They will count your known medals,
Even before the darkness unknown,
Suspending judgments, until your pen renews them.

New applauses throughout eternity

The edition of previously hidden lights
Shining on your distinguished desires, and lucid ideas
Of which displaying them, the author disapproves.

To him we owe more, but not easily

---

2 This epigram was dedicated to Spanish Noble and Knight, Don
Vincencio Juan de Lastanosa by Dr. Juan Francisco Andres, doctor
and friend of the author, as a way of thanking Don Lastanosa for
his patronage of Gracián and for helping in publishing his writings.
Without him, it is very doubtful we would have ever heard of Baltasar
Gracián.

His identity is indiscernible
His own name, he artificially hides.[3]

But because of you, his retirement results

In greater glory, and, in diligently disclosing
The subtleties of his cultured genius

---

3   Baltasar Gracián, who was known for preferring anonymity to fame, first began publishing his books under the pseudonym of Lorenzo Gracián (his supposititious brother) in order to remain unknown. He later went on to write under the pen name of Gracía de Marlones, after he was punished and censored for publishing *El Criticón: The Critic (1651-1657)* without his superior's permission. The only publication that bears Gracián's name is *El Comulgatorio: The Communicatory* (1655), which is a book containing meditations for before and after the Holy Communion.

To Prince Baltasar Carlos, Prince of Asturias[4]

Dearest Sir,

This happy affair, which friendship was able to make mine, I dedicate to you and consecrate to eternity. Small is the gift, but I am confident you will be satisfied with the prominence of flattery and the singular sweat of a scholar that is offered in this cult work. Emulation belongs to the hero, more so than a brother, in word and deed. Let this feather from an eagle be examined as we do the rays of the sun, which dawn so bright, the eclipse of the moon, and the withering of flowers.

Sir, Your Highness is the true Complete Man: commissioned to give to an imagined being life and the fame of a pleasant August summer.

—Don Vincencio Juan de Lastanosa

---

4   Baltasar Carlos was Prince of Asturias, Prince of Girona, Duke of Montblanc, Count of Cervera, Lord of Balaguer, and Prince of Viana. He was the heir apparent to all the kingdoms, states, and dominions of the Spanish monarchy until his early death at the age of 17 from smallpox. He was the only son of King Philip IV of Spain and Elisabeth of France.

First Approval

From Dr. Don Manuel de Salinas y Lizana, Canon of the Holy Church of Huesca

By commission of the illustrious Mr. Jerónimo Arasques, Doctor of Rights, Canon of this Holy Church of Huesca, Official and Vicar General of the most illustrious and most revered Mr. Don Esteban Esmir, Bishop of Huesca, of the Council of his Majesty, King Philip IV of Spain: *El Discreto: The Complete Man (1646),* published by Don Vincencio Juan de Lastanosa.

This literary work has cost me great admiration and careful reading, which was necessary to conclude that it has the most insightful wit; the distance between what the ear perceives to that which understanding penetrates, its wit quickly closes. Its title promises, and its words perform, and only the genius of an eagle could lift to success the difficulties of the matters discussed with such lucidity. All of the intricate matters which its author has achieved to elucidate (others undertake, he achieves) are exceptionally good, and I attribute this opinion not to affectation but rather to Gracián's presence as a force of nature; nature, in its understanding, always differentiates itself from the will, without which we are blind.

He shined the first lights of his ideas on the teaching of a prince, in *El Héroe (The Hero) and El Político (The Politician)*: lights which are akin to the sun gilding the summits with its first rays. The lucidity of his teachings is so eminent that he gives Art to Ingenuity, so as to convict your heart of wrongdoing if you ever walk unknown or new paths without them.

This book shapes a man of a general disposition into a complete man: but only if he understands that the former is an unpolished jewel of nature and that the latter is the result of polishing it with ingenuity and experience. It teaches a man to be perfect in everything, and that is why it does not teach everyone.

This work authorizes its doctrine with illustrations of distinguished men from all centuries, which are always needed as examples of virtue, courage, and magnanimity, in order to stimulate our weaknesses.

The style is laconic, and so divinized, and so sacred, that even its punctuations are mysterious. Measure yourself against the greatness of the matter contained in this book. Everything in it will get the approval of the knowledgeable, but it will not garner the applause of all because so few are discerning. It is a work, not to occupy the hours of the day but to achieve something meaningful in them; it offers little in the way of lecturing but much in the way of discourse. It does not contain anything against faith but rather revives it, because it excites the understanding of providence; nor does it contain anything against customs because it only tries to teach how to improve them. And so it can be given a license to be printed.

This is my opinion, in Huesca, Spain, on the 30th of January of 1646.
—Manuel de Salinas y Lizana

In view of the approval of the Canon, Mr. Salinas, we give permission for *El Discreto: The Complete Man (1646)* to be printed.

—The Dr. Jerónimo Arasques, Official and Vicar General

Second Approval

From Dr. Juan Francisco Andrés

El Discreto: The Complete Man (1646) by Lorenzo Gracián, published by Don Vincencio Juan de Lastanosa, is committed to me by order of the illustrious Señor Don Miguel Marta, doctor in both rights, of His Majesty's Council and Regent of the Royal Chancellery of the Kingdom of Aragon, so that I may express my feelings and assure you of the meetings of the royal preeminences, for the good of the republic, in whose pitfalls discretion is always very far from being endangered.

The matter he describes is so profitable, as those who carefully meditate on it will experience, that it is not enough to read it to understand it. The culture of his style, and the subtlety of his concepts, are so united with such a relevant connection, that it needs the attention of your careful prudence to take advantage of his doctrine. He flaunted the features of his arioso genius in *El Arte de Ingenio (The Art of Ingenuity)*, and in other works of equal artifice; but who will most admire the singularity of this idea, *El Discreto: The Complete Man (1646)*, if not his birthplace in Spain, Bílbilis (today Calatayud)[5], the motherland, Augusta Bilbilis, birthplace of the famous Roman poet Martial, who also inherits the ingenuity of nature? The constellations influence some climates more benevolently than others, hence the abundance of wisemen that are born in some places and

---

5   Baltasar Gracián was born in Calatayud, a municipality in the Province of Zaragoza, within Aragón, Spain, which the Roman Empire called Augusta Bílbilis. It was also the birthplace of Martial, the famous Roman poet. He is best known for his twelve books on epigrams and is considered history's greatest Latin epigrammatist.

the lack of wisemen born in others. Although this lack is often caused by the violation of genius by parents who allow their children to involve themselves in the arts and sciences, which they chose on a whim, without first finding out their true natural inclinations; from this cause, the misfortunes or successes of republics originate, as they easily falter when lacking wisdom and maturity; these are the political axes upon which stability is ensured.

Ignorance might be disillusioned in its errors, if it would put down malignity and come to know them; instead, it vainly demonstrates an attitude of superiority over others, seeking to advance itself and even persuade them, for it despises the observations of those who examine the propensities of the soul.

And so, in many provinces, these dictations of wisdom and the literary arts are practiced, but the men who profess them shine not with eminence but with mediocrity.

These mistakes can be corrected by those who observe the rules of this discrete diamond, because without discretion, he will be the same as a rough diamond, which, although it has intrinsic value, does not discover it until the burin engraves it, owing its brilliance more to the artificer than to its hidden radiance, and thus, it deserves to be given the stamp.

Huesca, Spain, 5th of February, 1646.
—Dr. Juan Francisco Andrés

Imprimatur[6]
MARTA Regens.

----
6   An *Imprimatur* is an official license by the Roman Catholic Church to print an ecclesiastical or religious book. This is where the stamp would have been placed on the original letter. The information directly under (spelled and written exactly as it is in the original letter) is most likely the title of the person placing the stamp.

To the Lecturers

From Don Vincencio Juan de Lastanosa

This is the fourth high-quality work that a personal friend has written and which I very proudly give to you. Many are missing, up to twelve[7], all of which aspired to so much emulation, but I can assure you that the present is not discouraged by the past. Certainly not his first work, which is about a Hero. Whose greatest glory is not in all of its fame; nor in having been printed so many times and in so many leagues; not in having been celebrated by the most cultured nations; not in having been honored so much, by so many writers, who inserted entire chapters of it into their learned works, but whose greatest glory is in being the product of this private Christian. His real applause, and even his life, were encapsulated in these real words with which the great King Philip IV of Spain graced him in a rare moment of praise: "This brinquiño[8] is very gifted; I assure you that he contains great things." That was the same as awarding him immortality. Even the royal crisis does not take away from him the celebrity that his second work on King Fernando the Catholic has attained, and which, until now, has been

----

7   At the time of this letter, Gracián had published four books: *El Héroe, El Politico, El Arte de Ingenio,* and *El Discreto.* He would go on to write three more before his death in 1658, producing a total of seven. We are told here that twelve are missing, so it seems Gracián wrote a total of nineteen books in his lifetime: the seven that were published, plus the missing twelve mentioned here.

8   Brinquiño is a small but very valuable piece of jewelry; King Philip is referring to Gracián as a very valuable jewelry box that contains great things—an uncharacteristic comment for a king to make and one considered beneath his dignity, so he must have been very impressed with Gracián.

considered his best work by judicious votes. Neither does his third work, the prodigious *The Art of Ingenuity*, which is so rare, erudite, and ingenious that those who read it cannot understand it, because until its publication, it had been considered impossible to find art in wit. It pleased a Genoese man so much that he translated it into Italian and even appropriated it, claiming it as his own. They are no longer content in taking the gold and silver out of Spain; now they want to take the wisdom out of her too! None, then, of those who precede him, nor those who follow him, even if they are attentive and gallant, will be able to surpass him in genius and ingenuity; he is the *ne plus ultra*.[9]

But I have heard two kinds of lecturers complain about his works: some complained about the material that it contained, and others complained about its style. The truth is that the former complain because of the excess of esteem that it has garnered, and the latter complain because they are not capable of matching its style. The first ones object to such sublime materials, worthy of heroes alone, and thus vulgarize them with the stamp of a commoner, selling them for the price of one Spanish real, so that they can spoil that which they are not capable of creating.[10] The second type of lecturer complains[11] that this punctual way of writing, with its concise style, spoils the Spanish language and destroys

----

9   *Ne Plus Ultra:* Latin phrase meaning "no more beyond." Here, Don Lastanosa says Gracián is the *ne plus ultra*: no other thinker, before or after him, will be able to surpass his intellect or wit.

10   Don Lastanosa seems to charge some lecturers with sabotage, claiming that they purposefully mark Gracián's books with the stamp of commoners and sell them at a very low cost, so as to discourage lords and noblemen from buying them or taking them seriously.

11   These lecturers were early critics of *conceptismo*, a literary movement of the Baroque period in Spanish literature, of which Gracián is considered a master and its leading exponent.

its clarity, which they call pure. Oh, how the critic Barclay[12] would formalize this vulgar charge if he heard it and add it to his famous work of satire, wherein he passionately condemns Spanish writers to barbarity for their plainness.

I will try to answer both of these complaints at once, satisfying each with the other, so that the first objection is a solution for the second and the second for the first. I say, then, that no one writes for everyone, and that is why the mystical nature of its style increases the veneration for the sublimity of its contents; the mysterious manner in which they are said enhances the reverence for its ideas. Aristotle and Seneca did not spoil the two languages, Greek and Latin with their writings and hidden meanings. On the contrary, they affected them so as not to vulgarize both philosophies, the natural one[13] and the moral one[14], even though these useless momos[15] cannot even understand them, much less tell them apart.

Make yourself deserving, discreet lecturer, either because you already are or so that you will be, of this art of connoisseurs and these aphorisms of prudence; use them to your taste and to your advantage.

—Don Vincencio Juan de Lastanosa

----

12   John Barclay was a Scottish satirist, Latin poet, and cosmopolitan man in the 17th century. Barclay's *Euphormionis Lusinini Satyricon*, which Don Lastanosa mentions here, was a severe work of satire on Jesuits, the medical profession, and contemporary scholarship, education, and literature.

13   A reference to Aristotle's "natural philosophy," which spans a wide range of natural phenomenons, including those now covered by physics, biology, and other natural sciences.

14   A reference to Seneca's "*Epistulae Morales ad Lucilium*" (Latin for "*Moral Letters to Lucilius*"), also known as the *Moral Epistles and Letters from a Stoic*, a collection of 124 letters.

15   "Momo" is Spanish slang for idiot or clown. It was used in the original letter by Don Lastanosa.

Acrostic Sonnet to the Author

From Dr. Don Manuel de Salinas y Lizana, Canon of the Holy Church of Huesca

Benjamín of Minerva, no longer in vain
The name that tries to rescue the world.
Lauro, the laurel, which the native lays
To crown you and flaunt you more proudly.

Man who, humble, triumphs with his hand
Matters hide from people,
Requesting more of your lucent rays
To the applause from the sovereign Apollo.

The coat of arms of El Discreto: The Complete Man
Enjoy your fame already, which is like light
That breaks through the air when your name is published.

Attentive and masculine, the perfect man,
You will rise in press quicker than anyone,
More than twelve and counting,
You are alone in greatness
North of the ingenious and laurelled alongside Apollo.

Explanation of the Sonnet

From the translator, Mr. M. San Pedro

This sonnet was written in the Spanish literary style of *conceptismo,* which calls for wordplay, witty metaphors, allegories, and descriptions of the matter through concepts rather than direct writings on the matter. In light of this, I have elected to explain the meanings in this sonnet for the non-specialized reader.

1. A) The canon refers to Gracián with an allegory, calling him "Benjamin of Minerva." The name Benjamin in the bible means "son of the right hand," and Minerva is the Roman goddess of wisdom. The canon is stating that Gracián is the son of wisdom and stands to its right: a position indicative of sonship and authority.

B) He then says, "no longer in vain," implying that he has held this opinion of Gracián for some time now and that his works and fame have finally confirmed it as true.

C) "The name that tries to rescue the world:" here, the canon compares Gracián to wisdom which the world and its inhabitants desperately need in order to rescue themselves from evil.

D) It then says that Spain, referred to here as "the native," is so proud of him that it lays a laurel around his neck and shows him off to the world.

2. Here, the canon uses another allegory to say that Gracián's knowledge and wisdom, when applied via writing on matters that are hidden, are like rays of light which shine on the truth to the satisfaction of Apollo, the god of discernment and truth.

3. Coat of Arms were used to establish identity. Here, the canon suggests that wisdom and fame now identify Gracián, especially after he wrote this work, *El Discreto*. He also writes, "Enjoy your fame already," alluding to Gracián's stubbornness in remaining anonymous, often publishing under a fictitious name so as to avoid any attention.

4. The canon showers Gracián with adulation and tells him that his wisdom has made him the perfect man. "More than twelve and counting," a reference to all of the books Gracián had written up to that point. He then says Gracián is worthy of standing next to Apollo, the god of discernment and truth, which is the same as saying his wisdom and genius matches that of a god.

EL PADRE BALTASAR GRACIA

A Man of Genius and Ingenuity

Commendation

There are two companions in life that will serve you faithfully if you cultivate them through habit, and they are genius and ingenuity, that is, your intellect and cleverness. They are stronger than Hercules and Atlas combined, and they will serve as the foundation of your brilliance.

One without the other results in half-hearted happiness, arousing envy, or the carelessness of luck.

Intelligence is always in season, but that season can be cold and damp without the enhancement of a pleasant character and genial inclination; and, conversely, good character can make a lack of intelligence that much more reprehensible.

Some wise men, far removed from vulgar tastes, say that having a happy nature is contingent on possessing the right type of intellect, and they confirm it with *etymology* (the study of the origin of words): for genius is said to come from ingenious. But experience serves us faithfully and teaches to the contrary, showing us the monsters in men when these two are totally reversed.

Every circumstance has a blade and a handle. The best and most useful tools, if seized by the blade, will wound you. But even the most destructive weapons, if seized by the handle, will serve you. A lot of what brings confusion and pain, if understood properly, instead brings enlightenment, because all circumstances have advantages and disadvantages. Some see everything as good, and others see everything as bad; use your genius and ingenuity as a compass and map that lead to the clarity and protection of moderation.

They are an ornamental worship of the soul, cultured enhancements, and they are admired by all, the crown of perfection. What the sun is to the greater world, they are to the lesser world; and they are even capable of imitating Apollo, the god of discretion. Every advantage in understanding heavenly matters comes from imitating the divine; if you wish to perfectly understand genius and ingenuity, emulate genius and ingenuity.

Through his abilities, man evolved from his brutish nature to become a little lower than the angels. And this confirms that we were made in the image of God and the divine. This becomes even more obvious when we consider our superior ability to understand and reason in comparison to other living creatures.

Yet, between one human and another, there is sometimes almost as much distance as there is between a man and a wild animal; if not in substance, then in circumstance; if not in liveliness, then in personality.

Once a sage looked at the sly fox and exclaimed, "Oh, she is beautiful, but she has no soul! I find in you the emptiness that so many wise men considered impossible." Sagacity looks at things from the inside; it is not deceived by apparent beauty; it gilds ugly foolishness; and if it is silent, it will be able to deny from the simplest of brutes to the most cunning of them, preserving the skin of its appearance. Silence has always cured foolishness, as the silent are seen not as lacking content but as being cloaked in a mysterious intelligence.

As for character, it was once considered a courageous spirit and sublimated to a deity, at a time when Chronos[16] was both lame and blind. The ancients considered it to be a *daemon*[17], thus exaggerating its importance. But now we have the light of Christianity, which speaks only of character's superior inclinations, which promise good things.

The creation displays God's genius and ingenuity, and it serves as a constant display of his radiance. It is to your benefit to cultivate these two faithful companions; in doing so, you will reflect the perfect God that created you.

Let genius then be singular but not anomalous, seasoned but not paradoxical, and judiciously displayed so that it may be admired as much as desired. May your ingenuity be a reflection of your condition, for even the heroic is not found in all kings, nor prudence in all who are discreet.

These fraternal twins are born of a sublime nature and favored in all causes. They prepare their master by seasoning his temperament in preparation for the highest state of mind, the readiness to deal with bizarre affairs, and the choice of glorious associations. They are delectable to the man who possesses them; this cannot be exaggerated!

----

16   Chronos is the Greek god of time. He is depicted as lame, and that is why he is slow. Here, Gracián says he was also blind, meaning that he existed before man's enlightenment by Christianity.

17   *Daemon*, (in ancient Greek belief) was a divine or supernatural being of a nature between gods and humans. The ancients believed that courage was a *daemon* assigned by the gods to each person at birth to accompany them through life.

Genius is not for all jobs, nor are all positions for ingenuity, whether superior or vulgar. No one person is suited for every occupation. Perhaps he will find one to be agreeable and the other to be repugnant, or perhaps both will be unfavorable, whether in terms of conformity or inconvenience.

Passion often deceives, and obligation can shuffle him between many areas of employment, so as to end up confusing and misplacing his talents until one day he finds himself fencing with a toga on. Chilon's[18] aphorism thus rings true:

"Get to know yourself before applying yourself."

The first step in molding yourself into the Complete Man is getting to know yourself! Alert your Minerva[19], show grace to her discursiveness, and give her encouragement if she is timid. But remember, it is always unfortunate to violate sanity by impetuously going against one's current state of taste, ingenuity, and luck; sometimes, doing so can be fatal.

Rome itself was not for everyone, whether genius or dunce. Nor is every culture given to all people to enjoy. Whereas one person may cherish a particular city, place, or setting, another may prefer to be alone in exile over living in the other's most beloved location. Even the great city of Madrid, known under the rule of the great King Philip from the East to the West for being the mother of the world, is recognized by some as a wretched stepmother and viewed with detestation. Oh, what great happiness it would be to stumble into each one and quickly distinguish its center! Rooks do not nest well among the muses, nor do wise men find

----

18   Chilon of Sparta is considered one of the Seven Sages of Greece.

19   Minerva is the Roman goddess of wisdom, strategy, and victory. Here, Gracián advises you to prepare your wisdom but also not get frustrated or rush the process of molding yourself into the Complete Man; doing so can deplete your sanity.

themselves in the busy capital, nor do the sane entertain political discourse.[20] Not everything is for everyone.

Certain settings will bring out more antipathy toward the secular world than others. This is most evident in large cities, where improprieties are standard and decorum is frowned upon. Some places you will relish, while others will bring out an uneasiness in you. Making yourself bear these settings, which run contrary to your disposition and intellect, will cause you great torment.

It is great luck to run into men of your same genius and ingenuity who share your values, interests, and culture. It is an art to know how to look for them and how to keep them. Blessed are those who bear the fruits of conversation, time spent, and happiness, which come from their acquaintance with likeminded geniuses—even more so when that genius is singular, excellent, or preeminent. For his latitude is infinite, as far as the north is from the south, as goodness is from malice, as sublimity is from vulgarity, as the sane is from the capricious, or as the remarkable is from the common.

Inestimable happiness comes when the preciousness of luck gives rise to the freedom of choice, which is seated to the right of genius. Ordinarily, however, the former comes forward to decide and to determine most opportunities, riches, employment, and other matters of import. It determines matters of the heart, affecting family, friends, servants, and even consorts, all without consulting with genius; for this reason, there are so many complaints from those who live

----
20   Rooks are a type of bird found throughout Western Europe, and Muses are sister goddesses in Greek mythology. Rooks are highly social birds; the males and females pair bond for life. In contrast, muses were often spoken of as unmarried and partnerless. Here, Gracián tells the reader that he needs to know himself intimately so that he does not find himself where he does not belong.

punished, in forced prisons, dragging all of their lives the mistakes of others. What is preferable then, in the case of its scarcity, and what is advantageous in the case of its excess? The brightest genius, to lift you out of poverty, and the cleverest ingenuity, to bring you moderation in times of excess; the latter of which leads to cautious judgment.

Assiduousness improves them, and impropriety rejects them. The greatest happiness is to engage them in their heroic nature, which is a bypass for good souls. Many lords have failed to experience this happiness by missing the vocation of their genius and of their ingenuity.

Let one and the other be enriched by extremities in virtue and in all that is good and true, so as to shine light into the darkness of the world, and may they crown you a prodigy, a prince, and a lord at all times, second only to the great king, King Charles V[21], who has known no equal neither in life nor in death; only he is first. Oh, glorious hope! That such a florid spring may offer us a July of courage and even an August of happiness![22]

21　King Charles V is generally considered to be the greatest king in history. As Emperor of the Holy Roman Empire and King over much of Europe, including Germany, Austria, Spain, and parts of France, he was the only man to rule both the Old and New Worlds.

22　Writers from northeastern Spain often used allegories referencing the summer months of July and August in order to describe something pleasant and happy, as this region tends to have its best weather during that time of year. For example, in the foreword of this book, Don Lastanosa mentions "the fame of a pleasant August summer."

‑II‑

A Man of Lordship in Words and Deeds

Academic Discourse

It is the natural humanity of Pandora to which Hesiod alluded in his allegory on her. She was not given wisdom by Pallas, nor beauty by Venus, nor eloquence by Mercury, nor courage by Mars, but rather faculty, which, with careful application, can advance one every day, driving one perfection after another. Jupiter did not crown her with the majesty of perfection in her thoughts and actions, which we admire in the divine, but rather gave her the arts of genius and ingenuity, which can only be mastered through self-possession and a magisterium only achieved with application.[23]

----

23   Gracián mixes Greek and Roman mythology in this allegory. Pandora, Hesiod, and Pallas come from Greek mythology, whereas Venus, Mercury, Mars, and Jupiter come from Roman mythology. Pandora was the first human woman, created at the instructions of Zeus, the Greek counterpart of Jupiter, the Roman god.

Here he says that, rather than receive superpowers, Pandora was given her own mind and freedom of choice. She held a box, known today as Pandora's Box, which she was not allowed to open because it contained all of the world's evil. However, she could not resist peeking into the container and, upon opening it, unleashed all evil into the world.

The interpretive meaning is that humans only have power over their minds and actions; without constant application of self-possession and Godly authority in our hearts (magisterium), we cannot master our words and deeds. Thus, we consequently unleash evil on ourselves and others through the careless exercise of our free will.

Most men walk in extremes. They either lack confidence or border on arrogance, the result of either their own nature and disposition or the malice and abuse of others. Sadly, low esteem gets a hold of them, and they believe they will not succeed in anything and that, regardless of what they do, their happiness and financial well-being will suffer at the hands of misfortune.

What is even worse is that they believe this without any proof. They find in everything something to fear, discovering first limits rather than conveniences. They surrender so much to this excess of pettiness that, not daring to act on their own, they make others timorous of their actions and even their desires. They are like those who do not dare throw themselves into the water unless they are supported by a safety raft, even when their feet can touch the ocean floor.

Others, however, are fully satisfied with themselves. In their conceit, they believe they can do no wrong and have never done any before. They are so satisfied with all of their actions that they have never doubted, much less regretted, anything that they have done. They are very happy with their judgments, yet the more so they are, the more erroneous they are. Like children, they are in love with their own speeches, but the more beloved they are, the uglier they are. Since they have no misgivings, they have no dissatisfaction either. To their understanding, everything goes well for them. And like this, they live very happily with themselves for a long time. Because of their narcissism, they have reached a very simple happiness that only the ignorant can know.

Between these two extremes of imprudence lies the sure means of sanity, and it consists of prudent audacity, greatly assisted by patience. I do not speak here of that natural superiority that we point out, like muscular enhancement or the natural lordliness I mention in *El Heroe: The Hero,* but of a sane fearlessness that is radiant, not dull. Rooted in the understanding of subjects and in the authority that comes with experience and maturity. The man who commits himself to this discreet audacity will be worthy of dignity, honor, and respect. The kind of praise that is reserved for accomplished kings and lords.

In the darkness that covers our world, riches grant authority. Gold often gilds the foolish actions of its owners, and silver communicates its silvery sound to words, so that the foolishness of a rich man is applauded while the astute sentences of a poor man are ignored.

But regardless, the most advantageous superior trait you can possess is Lordship in Words and Deeds, in the adequate knowledge of things and long experience in occupations. First you must become master of the subjects, and then you can enter and leave with grace, speak with masterly power, and say as a superior to those in attendance: "It is easy to master men, if one first masters knowledge."

With this Lordship, you will have adequate knowledge of things and the ability to continuously manage affairs. Through experience and study, one becomes a master of matters.

It begins with nature and is perfected through the application of genius and ingenuity. All those who attain these habits of lordship are prolific. The level of superiority it brings them allows them to meet great difficulty with great ease. Nothing embarrasses them, and they come out of everything with brilliance. They are able to profit even from the most painful of circumstances. Their deeds and their sayings are twice as good: any mediocrity seems like greatness, and everything is achieved with showmanship.

Those who do not have this superiority that Lordship offers them enter the circles of affluence with suspicion, which takes away much of their displays of greatness and even more if that suspicion is made known. From that suspicion then comes fear, which criminally banishes intrepidity, rendering you ineffectual. And any reason on your part is tarnished and even lost. Suspicion occupies the spirit, so that it is deprived of its noble freedom, and without that freedom, discourse is hindered, speech is frozen, and action is impeded. Without being able to act with the ease on which perfection depends, you soon find yourself outcasted.

The dominion of the Lord who speaks conciliates respect in the one who hears, makes a place for himself in the attention of even the most critical, and gains the acceptance of all. Lordship ministers words and even sentences to the speaker so that fear cannot chase him away. In his stream of eloquence, the coldness of fear will not overwhelm him.

The one who enters already possessing lordship in conversation and in reasoning earns respect beforehand and makes room for himself. But the one who arrives with fear condemns himself with distrust and confesses himself defeated; with this distrust, he gives rise to the contempt of others, even of those with low self-esteem.

It is true that the wise man must pause where he does not know, and more so when he does not know. Do not enter unreservedly and loquaciously, probing the depths of those around you, lest you fall victim to the negative attention of attentive males.

With princes, with superiors, and with all people of authority, it is necessary to reform your lordly audacity, but not in such a way that it leads to the other extreme of shrinking introversion. Here temperance is very important, taking care not to be angry at the daring or tarnished by the discouraged. Do not entertain fear, so that it does not succeed in appearing through your behavior.

Both apprehension and unchecked audacity will make you stand out. There are, however, conditions in people that make it necessary to enter with superiority, not only in cases of command but of request and supplication, because if some believe that they are respected or feared, they puff up and become intolerable. This behavior is common among those whom nature has humbled well and whom luck has failed to raise up. Above all, God save us from the vile pride of those in power.

The superior enhancement of lordship shines in all subjects, and more so in the elderly. The speaker is more than his subject matter. In a lawyer, it is his intrinsic nature. In an ambassador, it is his brilliance. In a general, his advantage. But used without discernment, lordship becomes a weakness.

The European woman is by nature lordly. What is nothing but a natural and innate lordship seems superb. The gravity of genius is born naturally, not of affectation. Learn to apply it and to command it well. Doing so greatly enhances all human actions, even countenance, which is the throne of decency. And your demeanor, which is the footprint of your heart, will be marked by judiciousness. You will act and speak with eminence, and the sublimity of your actions will be doubled by the majesty of just doing them.

Some are born with a universal lordship in all they say and do; it seems that nature made them dominant. They were born to be superior, if not for the dignity of office, then of merit. Infused in them is a kingly spirit, present even in the most common of actions, which sets them apart from their contemporaries. They defeat and surpass everything, then become masters of others and take their hearts. Everything fits in their great capacity. And although perhaps others will wear the more advantageous garments of science, knowledge, nobility, and even strength, they will not constitute as his superiors because of the lordship that lives in him. He will naturally rule over them, if not by birthright then by possession.

Others come out of the wheel of their clay already destined for the servitude of others, lacking the spirit of lordship in their hearts. They incline themselves to please everyone and to give their own to all as if it were of no value. These people were not born for themselves but for others; they are like a shadow that belongs to everyone who stands in it. Oh, how many have been made superior by luck, clothed in dignity, and blessed by nature but have made themselves slaves to fear and money!

Lordship is crowned with royalty, as if he were a king who ruled over others. Thus, he carries with him a great entourage of precious jewels. Whoever wants to admire them all together will find them in the most excellent Lord Don Fernando de Borja, the Spanish noble from the House of Borja and the House of Castro.[24] He was the third Count of Mayalde, Viceroy of the Royal House, and Prince of Esquilache. Firm in the grip of his right hand were prudence, integrity, and Christianity, all of which made him a beloved father in Aragon, a venerated man in Valencia, and a favored subject of the great king, King Philip IV, who entrusted to his prudent, majestic, and Christian discipline the most important thing: his own son, so that Lord Borja

---

24   Lord Don Fernando de Borja was a Spanish noble in the service of King Philip IV who was made the *Sumiller de Corps* of his son, the Prince of Asturias, Baltasar Carlos. He was the officer most responsible for the prince and was always in direct service to the monarch.

would teach him to be a king, a hero, a phoenix, and an emulator of the celebrated Achilles.[25]

But remember, although kings and queens may venerate you for your genius, be very careful not to tarnish it by weaving the defects of this world with your virtues. Greatness can and will degenerate through excess, affectation, imprudent recklessness, abhorrent entertainment, vain satisfaction, and other such things. Always follow the fatherly guidance of discretion and moderation.

---

25   In Greek mythology, Achilles was a hero of the Trojan War, the greatest of all the Greek warriors, and the central character of Homer's Iliad.

III

A Man of Patience

An Allegory

In a chariot and on a throne, the latter made of tortoise-shells and the former pulled by the most elegant horses, the Man of Patience waits and walks through the spacious fields of time to the Palace of Occasion, to finally experience that for which he has been waiting.

He proceeds through life with a majestic pause and displays the workmanship of maturity without ever becoming hasty or passionate. He reclines on two cushions presented to him by the night: silence and wisdom. In their counsel, he finds the greatest calm. His heart is like a sea, with its floods of passions, wherein the most furious tempests are contained, but all without roaring, without breaking its waves, without throwing up foam, and without going beyond the limits of the boundaries that his Lordship has set. In the end, patience makes all of him great in every way. The Man of Patience displays both great depth and great capacity.

His uniform is not one of pageantry but of decency, perfectly fitted and decorated with decorum. Its color is that of hope, and with it he brings relief to the most despondent without ever having to say a word. Among all colors, he positively hates rage, because it is symbolic of, first, the burning of his anger and, second, the subsequent embarrassment it causes him. Subtly in life, if you want to be a winner and a king, whoever masters the dissimulation of his attributes with prudent morality, so as to not draw unwanted attention, knows how to rule.

Prudence leads him to stand before antiquity's pillars of patience for advice, for there is wisdom in the multitude of counsel. Almost all of these pillars of patience are men, and on a few rare occasions, they are women. He patiently learns from them, for great knowledge always requires a long passage through time. These advisers carry the staffs of elders and pilgrims; others carry canes, swords, and crowns. The majority are men of nobility and rulers of kingdoms, most of them European. Europeans tend to occupy the best positions, not so much because they have been lords of the world, but because to be lord of the world means to be superior: in taste, thought, judgment, and will. They are Italian, Spanish, and a few French, as well as some German and Polish. The shrewdness and wisdom of the latter two comes more from the ice in their veins than from the alacrity of their spirit. There remains, however, a large empty space that had been occupied by the most prudent English nation, but since Henry VIII, it has lacked the triumph of sanity and integrity.[26] The Asians also stand out for their creative wisdom, prudence, and taciturn disposition.

These great men were made famous by this crowned quality and rode through life on its triumphant chariot. Here is the great Roman General, Fabius Maximus, who gallops through history on the iron horse of self-mastery. Through great forbearance, he restored the Roman Republic and vanquished

---

26   Henry VIII was known for his six marriages, sending two of his ex-wives to their deaths on the executioners block in the Tower of London, and for initiating the English Reformation: separating the Church of England from the Catholic Church, when Pope Clement VII refused to have one of his marriages annulled.

the gallant Hannibal Barca, the great Carthaginian General and Statesman. His legacy of patience has been venerated by even the best of military generals and is referred to as the "Fabius Strategy."

At his side stands the great English warrior and champion, King Richard the Lionheart, with his sword in his right hand and the crown on his head adorning the intrinsic jewels of patience. He was captured by the Duke of Austria, imprisoned, and later betrayed by his brother to King Philip II of France. He patiently endured his imprisonment and, once released, confronted the French king in battle and defeated his army.

And we cannot forget, El Gran Capitán, The Great Captain, General Gonzalo Fernandez de Cordoba, famously known for his exploits during the Italian Wars. For almost nine months, he showcased great patience and acumen under the greatest pressure, as a much larger French army formed a blockade in the Port of Barletta, surrounding him and his men. Under the most extreme of circumstances, this great captain held off the French forces and patiently waited until 6,000 Spanish troops arrived as reinforcements. He defeated the French army, killed the Duke of Nemours, collapsed the French position in Naples, and forced them to retreat. Great patience, ingenuity, and judgment earned this magnanimous Andalusian an entire kingdom. He conquered more with patience than with bravery.

There are many other examples, some of philosophers and scholars, exemplary professors and experienced teachers, all of whom slowly forged a golden crown from the chains of time.

Time governs victory; sometimes, stumbling around on crutches and being forced to take your time is in your best interest. Seasoning yourself, leaning on council, thinking, and maturing. Sometimes, we have to take a step back to leap forward. Those who refuse to submit to time end up like a furious squadron of monsters, heavily armed with impertinence, who forcefully impose themselves and bathe in the extremes of passion, indiscretion, reckless acceleration, foolish facility, and vulgar outrage. Impatience, impetuosity, and haste will always drown you in a sea of defeat.

We see this in the Battle of Alcântara, between Dom António and the Duke of Alba, Fernando Alvarez de Toledo. After King Sebastian was killed in battle, Portugal was plunged into a succession crisis, and King Philip II of Spain quickly sent an army to seize the throne. Dom António, who lacked support from the Portuguese nobility and high clergy, made haste, and began to recruit an irregular army composed of peasants and townspeople to face the Spaniards. However, the Duke of Alba met little resistance in battle and, within thirty days, captured Lisbon. Soon after, King Philip was crowned King of Portugal, while a defeated Dom António, exiled in France, fell into poverty and died.

"There are souls," the great king, Don Juan II once said, "dedicated to waiting, and mine is extremely so, and also dedicated to Prudence." Patience leads the Complete Man, who is a lover of prudence, and surrounds him with the spirit of greatness; it will always vanquish bravery, because humanity is very impatient and stupidity is very bold.

What is well said is briefly said. His Eminence, the wise Catholic King, King Fernando II of Aragon, understood that self-restraint is the foundation of patience and the principle of victory. "The one," he said, "who lords over himself will lord over everyone. Delay seasons success and softens difficulty, while reckless acceleration always gives birth to regrets, which are the lifeless abortive children of immortality. You have to think slowly and execute quickly; diligence not born of thoughtful delay is dangerous. As soon as it reaches for things, they fall out of its hands, a reminder that it should never have taken them. Waiting is the fruit of big hearts filled with courage and catalyzes very fruitful successes. Men with small hearts do not have the courage to wait and walk with time."

He concluded with this Catalonian oracle: *Deu no pega de bastó, sino de saó* (God chasteneth not with a rod but with time).

The greatest of kings, the triumphant King Charles V, used time to his advantage and became the only king in history to be the emperor of both the old and new worlds; he was the Emperor of the Holy Roman Empire, Archduke of Austria, King of Spain, and Lord of the Netherlands as the Duke of Burgundy. He knew that the crutch of time would affect him more than the iron club of Hercules. Wise was the sage who said, "Time and I against any two."

The judgment of disappointment is present when the virtue of patience is absent.

IV

A Man of Gallant Generosity

A Memorial for Discretion

I, Gallantry, can be found only in the human soul, and only I can make the Complete Man above average in comparison to his contemporaries. Determination of the spirit leads to gallant acts of the heart. I enable him to move through life with effortless grace. I make the eyes of his soul capable of searching the hearts of men, making his discernment sought after, praised, and flattered.

I dress in generosity. Among the common and universal, I am easily highlighted because of my magnanimity. This is even the case in the presence of villains, where I speak well with my enemies; with a faithful disposition that is supported by Christian teachings.

My greatest maneuver is keeping the man who possesses me from falling prey to the spells of revenge and envy, which present themselves in everyday circumstances and overcome so many. He does not ignore them but rather uses them to improve himself, turning opportunities for revenge into unthinkable acts of generosity and overcoming envy with wisdom. And although he cannot hear nor see the divine, heaven showers him with cheers and praise.

Emperor Augustus possessed me when he overcame the temptation of revenge and triumphed gallantly in the public's perceptions, making for himself an even more memorable greatness by not arresting his detractors and instead letting the poison of their tongues serve as their own judgment and prison.

The Complete Man's sphere is one of generosity, which blazes out of a great heart in both personal and business affairs. This is the maxim of divine faith, anchored by holy gallantry.

This was the path that led King Louis XII to immortality. Those who had insulted him when he was the Duke of Orleans feared his succession to the throne. But his discretion turned vengeance into gallantry with these inestimable words: "You have nothing to fear; the King of France does not avenge the injuries done to the Duke of Orleans."

The man who possesses me does not admire himself for his victories over revenge and envy. Although he seeks to be the greatest emulator of the great men who found themselves in similar circumstances, he never speaks of having conquered because he has nothing of pretension. And when he triumphs through merit, he attributes it to luck.

At times, he makes others feel indebted to him by refraining from taking that which he could claim. He is notable when unnoticed and great when slighted, though he cannot always turn disdain into politeness, for there is no way to repair the cracks of slander.

He uses gallantry and discernment to usher himself out of tight and compromising situations, usually with a simple word or deed, a joke, a maxim, a quip, or a paradox.

This was the case with the valiant warrior Don Alonso de Aguilar[27], when King Fernando III was staying at his palace: King Fernando complained that the stairway was too narrow, to which Don Aguilar responded, "Your Majesty, I never dreamed I would have such a great guest."

With me by his side, he transforms into kindness what would otherwise be a vulgar slight, and he does this from the heart, not for public consumption, for acting in counterfeit leads to infamy and welds you to artifice and trickery.

I am also an extraordinary shield against assaults, helping with remarkable dexterity against the attacks of mockery and in the defense of truth. With a courtly retort, whether of a nickname or of a sentence, I can often create a way out of a serious problem. With me, you can get out of even the most confusing labyrinth with grace.

It has always been a great feat of subtlety and art to show off insults and to turn those disgraces of nature and of misfortune into your own personal enhancements. Self-deprecation takes heroism, and, contrary to self-praise, he who learns this heroism will ennoble himself. What is condemned by the neglect of good behavior is easily disguised by the gallantry of this art. But always with temperance, soft words, and a soft spirit.

Together, gallantry and discretion can make any good action seem more graceful and supply a good excuse for any suspicious act, making them seem like charming mistakes, nothing more than the pardonable result of boldness. They make

----

27   **Don Alonso de Aguilar was a Spanish knight in the service of the king and saint, King Fernando III of Castile and Leon. He fought alongside King Fernando during the battles of the Reconquista to free Spain from the invading Moors and also served his father, King Alfonso IX.**

a king's caution seem humane and a priest's timidity seem like courtly caution. What others would condemn as poor decorum, they dismiss as unworthy of serious attention, but always with moderation so as not to fall into frivolity.

When they meet, they enhance the man who possesses them. And when they are eternalized in his reverence for God, the most noble greatness will be produced in him, which will take him into monasteries and palaces and lead him to accomplish great feats. And all this with prodigious gallantry, achieving the immortal crown of the extraordinary, magnanimous, and heroic. In the end, he will be buried in a memorial of merit, clothed in the garments of immortality and virtue.

V

A Man of Discernment

Academic Reasoning

More triumphs can be won with discernment than with courage. With the latter, one defeats monsters like Hercules did, but with the former, one confounds the wise and the proud with the golden chains in his mouth, condemning them to the sweet eloquence it produces in him. In the end, more is yielded with the gift of discernment than with the heart of courage.

Discernment gives one a certain courtly wisdom, polished conversation, and erudition that will make him well received everywhere and even eternally sought after with curiosity.

It is a virtue that is not taught in books nor learned in schools. It is learned in the theater of quietness, in the company of wisdom, and in the constant exercise of good judgment and discretion.

It will lead one into the arms of greatness, before men of influence who appreciate all that is well said and observe all that is gallantly done. Men who are knowledgeable of everything that is current in the courts and in the campaigns of kings. Men who are oracles of wonder and masters of discernment. Discernment communicates to him through erudite conversation, giving him great insight into all discussions. Acumen and enlightenment are the treasures it bestows.

His greatest enhancement will be a judicious understanding of subjects, penetrating cognition regarding this present tragic comedy called humanity, and shrewd estimations of impeccable judgment regarding kings and heroes.

The Complete Man correctly determines every kingdom: their eminent men of wisdom, courage, prudence, gallantry, understanding, and, above all, their saints. He gives a place to each one of them, quantifying their eminence and appreciating their value.

He also takes judicious note of the paradox and extravagance regarding individuals: their vulgarity and affectations. And, with precise calculation, he surmises their internal anatomy, conceptualizes their hearts, and gives proper credit to the truth. This superiorly cultured cognition serves him to better see and appreciate the facts of a matter, always using circumstances and interactions as a learning opportunity to the admiration of those nobles who are in his presence.

Above all, he is, through the love of wisdom and habit, a seasoned and mystifying copy of all the good sayings and gallant deeds of antiquity and of those heroes whose spirit still lives on today through their deeds. The sentences of the prudent, the malice of the critics, the wit of the charismatic, and the gallantries of the great captains are all sweet ammunition to conquer life. He keeps an aura of freshness by understanding modernity, its flamboyant facts, and contemporary sayings, adding the novelty of what is presently fashionable to his excellent understanding of ancient times. Changes in application are necessary to avoid becoming stale. The greatest proverbs, deeds, and knowledge become tiresome when repeated too often.

This virtue of discernment is more useful and honorable in this life than anything you can learn in the most prestigious academic institutions. It is an art of fortune, of which, if heaven gives it to you, even a little will suffice. It does not exclude the other serious virtues such as wisdom, courage, justice, and moderation but rather assumes them as the basis of its enhancement.

Just as gratitude enhances the affluent, discernment enhances great eminence. It adorns in beauty all virtues, enhances knowledge, and guards against the ostentation of the soul. The people who excel in this are rare and not easily found. Imagine for a moment if no one had troubled themselves to discern, observe, and record the heroic sayings of Alexander the Great, the Roman Emperors, the Spanish Kings, or the Seven Sages; we would have lacked the greatest treasures of understanding: true wealth for a superior life.

There are men who are eminent in this gallant faculty, but they are so rare. If you ever find one, consider him a treasure. If you ever chance upon some brave genius of such discernment, which among thousands will be a few, do not waste the occasion. Enjoy the seasoned delights of his enlightenment and intellect. Learn to hunger after that which is ingenious and wise—those oracles of judgment and mastery.

Your own carnality always leads you to long for that which you do not have, whether it be to your betterment or worsening. With this, you can learn to create an opportunity for the pleasantness of knowledge by using this longing to develop an appetite for discernment. Always be careful that you do not, in your carnality, barbarously use your taste for knowledge to tarnish your soul by boasting of how much you know. Some men return from the emporiums of the world as barbarously as they left. They did not take with them a capacity for discernment and cannot learn from their experiences. Thus, they make themselves void of reason and genius, making short use of their observations, if any at all.

But the Complete Man, like the tasty bee, has prepared himself to drink the new nectar that he has extracted from experience and observation. Discernment is to him what manna is to the angels and ambrosia is to the gods: tasty food, for which the ignorant can never develop a palate.

These estimable tidings that wisdom brings are not found in vulgar people. For them, discernment will never leave its corner. Consequently, they will never see past the tip of their nose or beyond the present. And it is not just the vulgar but also those who derive their happiness from this secular world. They only take from life for themselves and have no regard for the deity or his prescriptions for the soul; very few things are more vile than this. Without discernment, they spend their lives in pointless speech and wasted understanding.

Hence, it is why many never master life nor gain an advantage over others. They only know what they see and hear, living life from a position of disadvantage, remaining as poor in understanding as they are rich in distasteful matter.

Half of life is spent in conversation, and the other half in observation. Having great discernment forms a delicious banquet of understanding and enhances the greatest judgment. Perhaps the day will come when you can showcase your learned lucidity on the subject of discernment; it will make your knowledge of it immortal.

VI

A Man of Consistency

Crisis

Vices are not credited for being found in great men, so their contamination is even more noticeable when they are present. The stain on a silk garment is more offensive than the stain on a sackcloth. It is the unequal ailment of greatness and vice in kings that is so displeasing. Sometimes this is by nature; in most cases, it is by affectation, sparked by their desire to win the applause of the secular.

In his worship of vice, he creates a rotting condition for his mind and soul. Moving through life with double-mindedness, he insults the divine with his lukewarm behavior, flattering today what he will abominate tomorrow. And in two immediate instances, he does not raise himself toward the stars but instead lowers himself into the abyss.

Deviating from standard comportment into the abhorrent and back again usually ends in loss, worsening your situation. This is usually the case when men are trying to avoid pain. This is why the Complete Man, with his mastery of self-discipline and consistency, is usually a winner. Some are strengthened by the same thing that causes weakness in others, because they know that the same change that tormented them today, will shower them with strength tomorrow. The formation of vice lies in the very origin of evil, from which double-mindedness and inconsistent behavior is birthed.

Oh, this master of discernment, how calmly he coasts through both the beaches and the marshes. How correctly he measures the gulfs! He is neither moved by elation nor does he yield to misery, for he knows that life is a constant state of change. And, with discernment as his sword, he knows no change will ever be his end.

Gross inconsistencies of behavior are due to a dearth of reason and leave you at the mercy of darkness, a fate that is least agreed upon. The ability to allow the divine to guide you through both the fortunate and unfortunate does not depend on luck or merit. It is a skill based on discernment that one must master to keep sane.

Let your comportment and articulations be consistent with the divine, so that your "yes" is yes and your "no" is no. In this way, you avoid displeasing the soul and wasting your time chasing nothingness.

It is an egregious fault to allow the mind to wander when it is exempt from the temptations of the world. Learn to exercise lordship over its desires and wanderlust.[28] The wise man is always the same, which is to the credit of his discernment. Through the power of his will, he violates the forces of temptation and affectation in order to remain consistent. But life will proceed with its changes of scenery and circumstances even then.

----

28   Here, Gracián exhorts us to exercise thought control not just when facing temptation but also in all mundane and everyday aspects of life, whether good or bad. In a later chapter, Gracián warns against "useless curiosity."

The divine allows these changes in scenery and circumstances in order to develop him into a well-rounded, wise man. As a jewel cannot be polished without friction, so too cannot his discernment and wisdom be enhanced without tribulation. Inconsistency is a hideous vice that is well-rebuked by the many.

Without daily discipline and consistency, men of indolence become another version of themselves. In public, they behave very differently than in private; in the former, they befriend all virtue; in the latter, all vice. In public, they embrace their virtues, but in private, they make war with them again. Consistency of integrity matters, especially when no one is watching.

Look at the more monstrous inconsistencies of Emperor Nero. He did not conquer himself but rather surrendered himself to vice and double-mindedness, leaving behind a legacy of evil and terror. What is yet unseen will be seen, and the evils you do not conquer in your heart will manifest in your actions.

The Complete Man is a conqueror of evil by nature, and every great victory over himself leads to perfection. But the man of vice and abhorrence can never be a conqueror of anything because he himself has already been conquered by the darkness of his vice and the repulsiveness of his comportment. His soul itself has surrendered to deterioration.

If inconsistency went from bad to good, it would be good. And if it went from good to better, it would be better. But it usually consists of decline, so that we always see evil from the front and good from the back. Evil comes and goodness goes; it is the nature of iniquity that makes it this way.

The same earth, proud in its mountains, humbles itself in its valleys and displays its greatest beauty in its great variety. The same weather that crowns the flowers with rain destroys them with frost. The whole universe is a universe of variety, which leads to harmony in the end. The Complete Man uses the variety of good and evil that he encounters for the purification of his sins, winning the favor of heaven.

All the ups and downs in life are uncomfortable. To maintain your sanity, you need to remain consistent in your commitment to discernment. To wander from vice to virtue and virtue to vice will hurt your soul and cause heaven to vomit you out. There are men so inconsistent in matters, so different between occasions, that they contradict their own reputation and confuse our esteem for them. At certain times, they speak as if they suffer from delusion. Today everything goes well for them, and tomorrow everything goes badly. Both their understanding of life and fortune suffer.

These spawns of derangement put on their heads today that which they will carry between their feet tomorrow, yet they have neither head nor feet. They rob their close acquaintances of peace so that all flee from them, referring them to those who are vulgar and to the caretakers of lunatics who will better understand them.

The sea of bitterness is filled with the inconsistent, those whom heaven cannot trust. There is great danger in lacking consistency, because in doing so, you become a victim to the crimes of free will. And, once victimized, your behavior will not be far removed from madness.

But the Complete Man lives in the eternal blazon of his firmness, in all that is excellent, in all that is shining, in all that is enhanced, in all that is cogent, in all that is blissful, and in all that is perfect.

He is always discerning, always consistent, and always heroic.

-VII-

A Man of All Seasons

A Letter to Don Vincencio Juan de Lastanosa

One should not always laugh with Democritus[29], nor should one always cry with Heraclitus[30], my most excellent Don Vincencio. Every action demands its season; they should not be shuffled, nor should they be singled out; time should be given to all tasks, used either to achieve or to spend.

There is a time for the serious and one for the trivial as well: your own time as well as someone else's. Prudent action always asks for its own season. It is neither to be hurried nor is it to be delayed. Due time is needed for all tasks, some of which may be accomplished and others of which may be passed. The Complete Man is the master of all seasons and sought after by all who are noble and wise. God has made man a compendium of all that is natural. Let your behavior be the same for all that is moral.

He is the lord of all tastes and is sought after by all discreet men. Unhappy is the man who declares himself for a single time, even the most sublime; for what if that time were vulgar or full of vice?

----

29   Democritus, known as "the laughing philosopher" because of his emphasis on the value of cheerfulness.
30   Heraclitus, known as "the weeping philosopher" because of his dislike for the human species and constant depression.

The soldier who only knows how to talk about his campaigns or the engineer who only knows how to talk about his constructions only steal the ear of the unitone and the attention of the impertinent; when out of their element, they are lost because they only know how to sing a single song. May God free us from these monsters of repetition who only know one manner and one matter.

Variety has always been beautifully pleasing and, before lords and nobles, flattering. There are some to whom you can only look to for one thing because they do not know anything else. Unfortunately, most people are so: people of a single word; snoozers of conversation who push their boulders up the slope of boredom and sweat. The Complete Man is often tested by these inerudite fools, who tax his patience with their conversations of nonsense. Knowing that judgment will pour out of his pores and fearful of such a painful contingency, he covets sterile solitude and lives inwardly, in a perpetual golden age. The ugliness of this world has a way of destroying that which is beautiful. Yet there are others who can always touch on a point and talk about a subject. They are men of wisdom, geniuses of conversation, whose minds ooze with theine.[31] Every prudent man rightly respects them, and the king's court is always in search of them.

Some people's abhorrent nature leads them to anger for the sake of being angry. But he, with good taste, loathes anger, and is self-deprecating. He is strict with himself and tolerant of others: a universal friend, a genius of wit, a man of all hours. He is always in season and always on occasion, but always living inwardly.

----

31 Theine: caffeine, especially as it occurs in tea; here, Gracián uses it as a metaphor for alertness.

One is worth many, and thousands are not worth one. His universality of will and understanding is born of a capable spirit with infinite ambitions. In possession of a great taste for everything that is not vulgar, he knows how to enjoy things and to achieve all that is good. His heart is full of reverence for antiquity, erudition, and plausible history. The discernment that makes this possible is greater than all the philosophy of the sane. But all of these are partial eminences that he must perfectly weave together to form a more perfect character.

The prudent should not be tied to a single use, nor determine their taste to be for any one single thing, unless they wish to condemn themselves to unhappiness. To do so goes against nature and the very God who created us. And reason bears witness to this truth. We know the divine is infinite and without terms; he is not reduced or limited, and we are a reflection of him, created in his image.

Great men are indefinable too because of their vast plurality of perfections, which they repeat infinitely. Yet others are so limited that their tastes are known; they never amaze or flatter, and whether they come or go is of no consequence to those around them. To always speak attentively causes anger. To always take chances causes distrust. To always philosophize bores, and to always criticize disheartens.

He lives in the palace of wisdom, before the presence of judgment and discretion. In the company of nobles whom he is accustomed to seeing, he behaves as if it were his first time getting acquainted with them. Before those whom he has never seen, he behaves as if they were family. He does the former so they do not consider their presence stale and the latter to communicate warmth.

His confidantes do not get in each other's way, nor do their tastes contradict one another. They all fit in one center, and for everything he makes a season. Some men have no time for others and always prioritize their own convenience. But not him; he has time for himself and for many of his select friends.

For everything except the indecent and degenerate, there must be a time and a season. It is an affront to those who highly esteem you to be considered wise by day but exposed as a fool by night; hypocrisy is an ugly garment that should never be worn.

Great performers can act in all parts of a theater production. Sometimes they bring you laughter; sometimes they make you cry. Sometimes they are sane, and perhaps other times they are fools. But regardless of the character they play, their appearance ends with relief and applause.

All lavish engagements find their place in the well-distributed taste of the Complete Man. His heroic universality is a place wherein all that is erudite, cultured, and prudent finds opportunity. He is the learned and the gallant, the religious and the gentleman, the humanist, the historian, the philosopher, even the most subtle theologian.

He is truly a universal hero for all times, for all tastes, for all engagements, and for all seasons.

A Man of Understanding

A conversation between
Dr. Juan Francisco Andres and the author

DOCTOR: The Complete Man is a man of few words.

AUTHOR: I would also say that he is a man capable of deciphering very much with very little information. But more importantly, he understands and interprets countenance, which is the door to the soul, and displays what is written in the heart of a man. Silence is the language of God. With it, he understands more than with a fool's prolixity.

DOCTOR: The truths that matter most to him always come half-told.

AUTHOR: Yes, but he lives inwardly, in the citadel of silence, and receives warning from his discernment.

DOCTOR: What about the truths that seem foolish to the world?

AUTHOR: Those no one wants to say, for fear that they will look insane. And those that do tell them are very rare, like relics cloaked in mystery.

DOCTOR: How does a prince navigate and find difficult truths?

AUTHOR: With the compass of reason; winning or losing depends on this.

DOCTOR: Those truths sound like a maiden, as modest as she is beautiful, and that's why she is always covered.

AUTHOR: Let the prince disrobe her with gallantry. Some truths require you to masticate on them, so that they are better digested and more useful. Other truths are disappointing and political in their nature. They walk between two lights, ready to retire into the darkness of flattery in order to avoid embarrassment or to come out into the light of truth when challenged by reason. His discernment will serve him as a diviner of truths and a handler of disappointments.

DOCTOR: I would love to see the verbal exchange between a wise man, who forewarned, and the person who did not heed his warning!

AUTHOR: Intelligence has to be adjusted to match the capacity of the audience it is speaking to. Understanding their countenance will tell you whether they are ignorant or rational, so you can adjust your intelligence. In hateful matters, a lot of the man is revealed in his slight frowns; anger is always very honest. Some will heed advice, and others will not, continuing instead to navigate with their compass of ignorance. In matters of the latter, it is advisable to stop throwing your pearls to the swine.

DOCTOR: In odious matters, I would think one would listen to a wise man.

AUTHOR: Understand that the wise man says more with a little silence than with many words. The discerning go into their tent and meditate on the glassy points of what he said and the energy of his silence. Those who lack reason will not do this.

DOCTOR: It is very difficult to be understood when you are delivering matters of disappointment, because what is not wanted is badly believed; conversely, it does not take much eloquence to persuade us to accept what we do want to hear.

AUTHOR: All of the wisdom of Solomon is sometimes not enough for us to accept what we don't want to hear, and some men seal their hearts and let things rot in their chests.

DOCTOR: In that case, do as the physician does and take the pulse of the subject in front of you by gauging his demeanor and countenance.

AUTHOR: It never hurts to know.

DOCTOR: Just as prudence notices what they do not say, sagacity has to observe what they do say. The path of life is insidious, with the deceitful Sphinx[32] lying in wait to ambush the one without discernment, who is lost. Man is an enigma and difficult to understand.

AUTHOR: There is nothing easier than the knowledge of others. Because you only have to look at your own reflection. The first step in knowing others is knowing yourself.

----

32   Sphinx: a winged monster with a woman's head and a lion's body. It propounded a riddle about the stages of human life and killed those who failed to solve it. Gracián refers to it in an allegory urging the use of discernment to solve the complexities of life and avoid falling victim to the iniquity of man and the evils of this world.

DOCTOR: Simple, but, at the same time, nothing is more vitriolic.

AUTHOR: There is no simple thing that is not malicious.

DOCTOR: Simple faults! Careful that they are not doubled by those of others.

AUTHOR: By perceiving the speck in a neighbor's eye?

DOCTOR: Yes! And not seeing the beam of your own.

AUTHOR: Truly, the first step of knowing is knowing yourself.

DOCTOR: He who does not understand cannot be understood. But that aphorism of knowing oneself is easier said than done.

AUTHOR: One will be counted among the seven wise men if he achieves this.

DOCTOR: The more some know of others, the less they know about themselves. The fool knows more about another's house than about his own. He talks a lot about matters that should mean nothing to him and nothing about the matters that should mean everything.

AUTHOR: Is there an occupation worse than leisure?

DOCTOR: Yes, useless curiosity!

AUTHOR: Beware of men who speak of things without substance!

DOCTOR: It is also necessary to distinguish between those who exaggerate and those who diminish. Discern then, as an attentive listener, the one from the other. Because many are those who have been condemned by both credulity and incredulity.

AUTHOR: That is why the Scythian barbarians wisely said that men are like rivers: some run wild, and others restrain themselves; the deepest tend to be the most calm, and those that make less noise carry more water.

DOCTOR: Finally, there are subjects in which suspicion matters as much as proof. In some, their words raise suspicion and doubt, while those same words serve as evidence and proof in others.

AUTHOR: The same words can mean more or less, depending on who is speaking them.

DOCTOR: One last thing, with respect to your comment that "men are like rivers." Many have drowned by simply wetting their feet; let the discerning person know that sometimes the best swimmer is the one who knows how to stay dry.[33]

AUTHOR: And more so if the water is purple.[34] And with this, we go into its history, if desired, with curiosity and enlightened erudition, and I, with my philosophy of *The Complete Man.*

----

33   Here, Dr. Andres uses an analogy to remind the reader not to get involved with just anyone and that many people have done themselves harm by "simply wetting their feet," which is another way of saying they became slightly involved with the wrong person and encountered great trouble (drowned) as a result. He advises avoiding such people completely (staying dry).

34   Extremely hard water is purple in color, as it has been calcified over time. It is very bitter and difficult to drink. Gracián is suggesting that some men, calcified by past experiences, are like this water: bitter and difficult to swallow, requiring great knowledge and philosophy to deal with.

-IX-

Humor and Propriety

Satire

Prudence is crucial, especially in important situations that conciliate the veneration of extremes; it protects your genius. A man who always jests is never a man you can trust. There are some who are always in mockery; view this to your advantage; with discretion, it will be easy to affect them, but always out of sympathy for their ignorance. Prudence is known for its seriousness, which wins more respect than wit.

Comedy must have its time, or it will create distrust in those around you. There are labels on goods that tell you how and when they are to be used. It is necessary to do the same with comedy, and even more so with people. To mock another is to treat him as an inferior, denying him of decorum and veneration. The man who is always joking falls short of perfection. No humor is worse than continual humor, because one never knows when the jester is exercising his judgment! Thus, it is the same as not having any at all.

Those who are always in jest are often treated with indifference and equated with liars. They never speak with discernment, and that is the same as not having it. Even worse, they are seen as being ignorant. Not because they do not showcase their judgment, but because they are perceived as simply lacking any. Society has convicted them of being defective in character, discipline, and will. They have only one goal, and that is to entertain and make people laugh, sometimes on purpose and other times inadvertently.

There is another kind of man who is even more annoying because he claims victimhood, as he is, at all times and with everyone, in quarrels. He cries out in pain even as he strikes you. An abhorrent monster from whom all flee, he tries to court with instigations and flatter with crumbs. He schmoozes and sugarcoats conversations in order to pry and snoop, so that he can find contempt in what others say. Murmuring becomes the vocation of his life, and in the process, he triggers a prodigious anger from heaven. He is given up to gracelessness and the abominable coldness that consumes him.

Indecent comedy causes you to lose credit as a man of discernment. When the pleasure of the joke has passed, the stain of its disgrace will remain—double if it was frequent. You will cry for your reputation long after you have made the others laugh. No one is spared from this fate, neither the most friendly nor the most composed. It is a serious defect born of men bankrupt in both substance and morality.

Men of greatness and destiny are measured. They know that vulgarity endangers decorum and destroys morale. And so those within their sphere of influence respect their judgment and reciprocate it with affection.

To some, it is connatural to have this generous genius. Nature endows them with this gift. And, when tempered with grace, it is a beautiful attribute without any defects. One little grain of gracefulness enhances even the most authoritative. Do not let yourself be overcome by secular inclinations that are born of sin, or you will end up a man seasoned with impropriety and ridicule.

There are some who, despite the deity's regret, force their humor. And since it is false in them, it raises annoyance rather than pleasure. If they manage to make you laugh, it is out of the coldness of their deviance. Through romancing your sense of humor, they seek to lower your resistance and pry information from you.

Affectations and artificialities are always irritating, and they are intolerable in jest because they insult the genius of your audience, leaving them offended and displeased. While wanting to make people laugh, they are left looking ridiculous. And if those who made themselves look ridiculous live in disrepute, how much more so do those who were affected by them?

There are those men who are graceful and those who are burlesque, which is a big difference. The Complete Man, who has mastered discernment, always sides with grace. He does not affect situations and instead waits for their due season. A grain of this salt, which heaven has estimated to be more valuable than pearls, is rarely dropped carelessly, saving sanity and asking decorum for permission.

Oh, the value of grace on all occasions! Grace is invaluable in difficult situations. It is the perfect seasoning for slights and snubs. There are slights that have to be taken as jokes, and perhaps some that are to be taken more seriously; only discernment can be a revelator.

The hardship of dealing with tactless men falls very heavily on the unsuspecting souls that cross their path. What agony it is to deal with these reprobates full of sinister wit who joke even about death itself! To deal with them is like trying to fall on a sword with grace. A difficult task? Yes. An impossible one? No.

Cato, the Roman senator and lover of freedom, preferred death to living under the authoritative hand of Emperor Caesar. He fell on his sword and, in doing so, became a martyr for Rome: poised, composed, and sane. His acuity and cogency in dealing with extremities won him the veneration of the centuries. It is not what one does but how one does it.

Fools always suffice for one another, either because they do not notice their ignorance or because they resemble each other. But the prudent man cannot violate himself; doing so disrupts his relationship with discernment.

There are moments for humor, but the rest of the time belongs to seriousness.

-X-

A Man of Decisiveness

Praise

All human knowledge (if, in Socrates' opinion, there is a knowledgeable human) is reduced today to the sound judgment of a wise choice. Little or nothing is invented, and any unfamiliarity in what matters most is to be regarded with suspicion. It seems as though we are at the end of ages with only new ways of being crass and indecent being created.

Back in the golden age, things were invented; nowadays, everything is repeated. All things are so advanced that there is nothing left to do but choose. Let us live then by the power of our choice, one of the most important favors of nature, perfected by the few; distinctiveness and excellence double its appreciation.

We see studious and knowledgeable men of subtle wit and judgment lose their way through poor decision-making every day. They always choose the worst, the least accurate; they prefer the least plausible, with its overtones of judgment and contempt for others.

Everything goes unhappily for them, and not only do they not obtain applause, but no one even likes them. They have never done anything distinguished, and all this is because they lack the great gift of knowing how to choose. Neither study nor ingenuity are enough where choice is lacking.

Its importance is transcendental because its extension is not less important than its intention. All jobs require its favor, and the greatest its affectation. The ability to choose wisely is the complement of perfection, the origin of success, and the seal of happiness. When it is lacking, circumstances and opportunity are tarnished and spoiled regardless of the abundance of artifice.

No one will ever achieve the credit of mastery in any undertaking without the enhancement of judicious taste. Only the enhancement of discerning choice could make kings eminently famous in their choices, both of companies and of ministers. So important is the power of discernment in choice that one mistake of reason is enough to lose everything and be discredited forever. And one success is enough to win everything and gain an immortal reputation. Some err in the choice of affairs, and others in the choice of moderation. They destroy the most precious gold of their crowns as a result of such fatal errors.

There are some occupations whose main exercise consists of choosing, and in these the dependence on decision is greater, as is the case for all those whose business it is to teach by appealing. Therefore, let the orator prefer the most plausible and serious arguments. Let the historian choose the sweetest lessons from the past and profit from them. Let the philosopher marry the specious with the moralistic, and let all attend to the universal taste of others, which is the rule of choice. Because in a banquet, the astute would prefer to please the guests over himself. What does it matter that things are very much to the taste of the speaker if they are not to the taste of the audience for whom they are seasoned?

-XI-

A Man of Moderation

Satire

Excellence in everything is very good, but too much use becomes abuse. It is coveted for its greatness, but too much of it makes it common, and in losing that first rare esteem, it achieves the contempt of the vulgar. It is a pity that its very essence causes its ruin. The applause of all is transformed into the anger of all.

This is the ordinary direction of excellence: very clear in every kind of eminence from which greatness is born, while simultaneously priming itself for its very ostentation. Without moderation, it will overthrow and even bring down the steepest greatness. It is enough to do well! But excessively showing off turns excellence into vulgarity.

It is a great defect to be a man who is for nothing. But so is being a man who is for everything, or wants to be. It is important to discern when to be for and when to be against. There are subjects whose excellence makes them sought after by all, and other subjects so abhorrent that everyone avoids them. Yet there is no subject, however repugnant to his genius, that cannot be affected by his direction or management. Everyone predicts a favorable outcome for all on which he lays his hands. And although he may not be looking for anything specific, his very excellence discovers them, and others seek to please him and expedite his convenience. Fortune favors him, making his opinions almost works of amusement. But this is more often than not random and can even end up being a defect. He can have a surplus of value one moment and be worthless the next due to too many victories.

Oh, the great sanity of a happy medium! If we could only know and restrain ourselves, then we could walk with assurance!

Admiration is like a very excellent painting of a most precious tapestry that is frequently encountered at a party. Everyone sees it when they walk in, while they are there, and on their way out. And, owing to the very attention it received throughout those numerous encounters, presto! It comes to be useless—or common, which is worse.

Then there are some who are neither few nor sane, who are exorbitant and excessive. Those who are always calling and seeking; they will stop sleeping and even eating to not stop doing. There is no present for them like a frenetic one, nor is there a better day than the busiest, and most often they do not wait to be called to interfere in everything. They add to the entertainment of an audience with affectations, which is to force foolishness; through great effort, they expose themselves to garner attention. But, right or wrong, they get everyone to talk about their hair, which is the same as controlling their tongues for gossip or contempt.

Although there is no further cause for disdain beyond that continuous encounter with them, always hearing about them causes such an angry weariness that they come to be as intensely hated as they were previously desired.

Not everything comes out of their hands with equal ease or in moderation, and what started perhaps as a great achievement, even through sheer luck, comes to a close in a beautiful vase of their own humiliation and discredit.

Those who want to please everyone, which is impossible, come to displease everyone, which is easier.

Those who are looked upon with envy or hate do not escape. The more they show off, the more those feelings are emulated. They all stumble on the scoff that protrudes from others. Decorum is like glass—brittle but delicate, and the ego is not known for self-awareness. When it is pleased with itself, it tends to want more exposure and more encounters, which only leads to more contempt. Better to preserve a reputation by retiring, even at the expense of self-esteem.

Some always want to be the roosters of publicity, and they sing so much that they anger those who have to hear them. They would benefit from advice or vigilance from a voice or two of reason. Then there are also those of beauty, whose flaunting, in addition to the risk, later has the punishment of dismissal and contempt. Unfortunately, those who are always singing and full of vanity are usually the most stubborn.

The second taste of the most delicious delicacy loses much of that first pleasure, and after three times, it becomes nauseating. Better to conserve the initial taste of fresh fruits and arouse desire. And if this happens with the tangible, how much truer is it in the true pasture of the soul, in the delights of understanding or refinement, and with delicate and ill-contented matters? Even more so!

How much of a good thing is too much is always a difficult estimate. It is better to go under than to offend by going over.

When an excellent man, whether his excellence lies in courage, knowledge, integrity, or prudence, retires, he becomes covetable because he removes himself while still loved and admired. All temperance is healthy, even more so when it regards ubiquity; this preserves life and reputation. A great skill is knowing how to make yourself esteemed, knowing how to sell your eminence, how to affect its concealment, how to preserve it, and even how to increase it if you so desire. Moderation is healthy, especially in matters of public appearance, where it conserves life and fame. The same applies to beauty: if you show it off on all occasions and combine it with everything as a signature move, you will be met with indifference and scorn. Most of the time, the value of a thing lies in its scarcity.

One woman who was a master of this was Emperor Nero's famous wife Poppaea; she understood how to make the most of her beauty without being offensive to others. She managed her appearance with great skill, playing her cards slowly, one by one, and even making herself envious of how good she was.

A great lesson, and one that I will teach in *Warnings to the Attentive Man*, is to know how to win esteem, how to sell one's excellence by covering it in order to preserve it, and even how to increase it by arousing desire.[35]

----

35   Aphorism 150 in Professor Christopher Maurer's *The Art of Worldly Wisdom*, the famous 1992 translation of Gracián's, *El Oráculo Manual y Arte de Prudencia (1647)*.

The famous story of the Indian and the emeralds confirms the aforementioned belief: He bought a large number of emeralds of equal quality. He showed the first to a lapidary expert, much to his appreciation and admiration. He then took out a second, a third, a fourth, and so on and so forth. Each increase in carats depreciated them. The very abundance of preciousness harmed itself, and as the rarity was lost, their value diminished.

Oh, Man of Discernment! If you want to earn an immortal reputation, be extreme in perfection but moderate in what you showcase.

XII

A Man of Temperance and Judgment

A Letter to Dr. Juan Orencio de Lastanosa, Canon of the Holy Church of Huesca, singular friend of the author

If I were to believe in fortune, I would also believe that its house was a house with two doors, one door being very different from the other and found in every aspect of life. One door is made of white stones, worthy of the happiest on the best day. The other, its opposite, is made of black stones, which, in their glare, portend their unhappiness. The former is majestically joyful, and the latter is gloomy and sad. Through the door of white stones there exists contentment, rest, honor, fullness, and riches, with all kinds of happiness. Through the door of black stones exist sadness, work, hunger, contempt, and poverty, all rooted in the lineage of misfortune. Therefore, one door is labeled pleasure and the other sorrow. All mortals frequent this house and enter it through one of these two doors. It is an inviolable law and one that you should observe with great rigor: whoever enters through one door must exit through the other, and no one can leave through the same door by which he entered. On the contrary, he who enters through the door of pleasure must leave through the door of sorrow, and he who enters through the door of sorrow must leave through the door of pleasure.

A common snub of fortune is to give very favorable entries and very tragic exits. The applause at the beginning makes the murmuring at the end even louder. The issue is not in the consent to an entrance, most of which are reasonable, but in the general feeling of an exit. Few people ever want to leave; desired exits are rare.

Oh, how many suns have we seen born with laughter at dawn and then buried with tears at sunset? The flattering robins greeted them at dawn with their songs, only to have the coyote ignore them at night with his howls.

All the facades of a structure may be ostentatious, but it is still humble in the back. The entrances of dignitaries are crowned with cheers and their exits with curses. Their commands are met with applause, while the hidden hopes for particular favors and common successes of their adulators are wrapped in malevolence; silence would be a more favorable acclamation.

How adored, either by hope or by fear, the valiant enter. But no one can deny the dictation of the divine. Although it may vary in privacy, he cannot escape at the beginning nor at the end from a predestined unhappiness!

The joys at the beginning are transformed into many discontents by the end. The sun rises with brilliance and sets with gloom. And in that sunset, deviations occur that darken its splendor and cool all affection. Happiness rarely accompanies those who leave, nor does the acclamation last until the end. As satisfaction is shown by those who come, displeasure is shown by those who go. Even friendships that are made with delectation are lost in ruination. All fly on favor and fall without it. It is also common in all jobs and business affairs to enter through the door of contentment and happiness and leave through the door of disgust and unhappiness.

Fortune is as courteous to those coming as she is rude to those leaving. Use extremes of prudence and fastidiousness to finish well, setting your sights more on the satisfaction of an acceptable exit than on the applause at the entrance. Palinuro[36] governs his vessel not by the bow but by the stern; there he assists in guiding you on the journey of life.

Some have very happy and reasonable starts in everything they do. They enter a place with acceptance, reach a position with applause, and begin a friendship with favor; everything they start begins with satisfaction and happiness. But these usually have very tragic ends that leave them embittered. All the unhappiness is left for dessert, like the bitterness at the end of a sweet bottle of wine.

A certain Roman[37] had a great rule regarding beginnings and endings: "Obtain all the dignities and positions before you want them, and leave all of them before others want you to." The former here is more a favor of luck, but the latter is more a matter of singular prudence. Perhaps misfortune is a punishment for intemperance and glory is a reward for anticipation. It is better to leave a thing than to have it leave you. Prevention is also advisable.

36　In Roman mythology, Palinuro is the helmsman of Aeneas' ship. Authors later used him as a general navigator or guide figure. Here again, Gracián displays his mastery of *Conceptismo*. After advising prioritization of a matter's end rather than its beginning, he then mentions a mythological guide who navigates a vessel by its stern, which sits at the end of the vessel. It is another way to say that it is better to navigate life by focusing on favorable endings, not flattering beginnings.

37　Gnaeus Pompeius Magnus, also known as Pompey the Great; a leading Roman general and statesman.

Learn to find contentment and to accompany it with good manners until you come to a good opportunity. Preserve it irrespective of the grace of the people, with such genius that the common acclamation that greets your entrance, becomes a universal feeling that accompanies your exit.

You must never end an association, be it a friendship, a job, or with another position, in a breakup, because all social failure brings penalty and offends reputation. People always remember the ending of a thing, but very rarely the beginning!

Very few lucky ones escape the final reversals of fortune, which usually still leave them with bad consequences in exchange for great happiness. Even fewer escape with luck, good consequences, and their sanity. Then there are the heroes, to whom the divine offers up heaven as a remedy, mysteriously enhancing their end, like Moses, who disappeared, and Elijah, who was raptured, making them triumphant over death.[38] And in Rome, with fabulous gentility, Emperor Romulus[39], who disappeared during a sudden and violent storm while he was reviewing his troops. He transformed his death into a mystery, which caused him even greater veneration.

Others, though eminent and even heroes, erased the glory of their deeds with the unhappiness of their ends. Hercules made scant of his own immortality when he donned the

----

38   This story of Moses is found in Deuteronomy 34, and the story of Elijah is found in 2 Kings 2.

39   Emperor Romulus was the founder of Rome. After a reign of 37 years, Romulus suddenly disappeared during a violent storm. Supposedly, as the winds grew more fierce, Romulus was picked up by a whirlwind and never seen again. The ancient Roman historian Livy states that Emperor Romulus was more than likely murdered by senators during the storm who were inspired by their jealousy.

poisoned cloak, which began to burn him, causing excruciating pain. Despite his efforts, Hercules was unable to remove the cloak. He then decided that death was preferable to suffering such pain and asked for help from the gods to end his life, and he received it. The Greek god Zeus sent lightning to consume Hercules' mortal body and took him to live with the gods on Mount Olympus. A matter of sentiment to the brave but disappointment to the wise. How something ends is more important than how it begins.

Virtue alone is the phoenix, reborn just as it seems to end, eternalizing in veneration that which began with applause.

XIII

Envy, Ostentation, and Discernment

Apologue

Prodigious are the eyes of envy, but if they had any sense, they would not want to see as much as they see; being the most perceptive without self-mastery means never having serenity. Oh! If only humans exercised as much sense as birds, who see and acknowledge the winged portent of beauty, the peacock, but do not compare themselves to him. They all look at him, feathered in the sun, rays of sunshine glistening on his bizarre wheel of plumage, with a touch of indifference.

One proceeds from looking to admiring, at least when there is no passion or ill will. But if there is, it quickly corrupts and, when it cannot reach emulation, transforms itself into envy. Better to be content, like the crow in his field, the eagle in his cliff, the swan in his pond, the falcon on his perch, the parrot in his cage, and the rooster in his coop; and we cannot forget the owl, happy in his gloomy attic. Emulate the phoenix, who flees from envy and keeps herself wise and legendary in retirement.

Then there is ostentation, the offspring of vanity. What begins as well-concealed self-praise usually ends in a declaration of complaint and murmuring by the ones who hear it. Greatness and gallantry cannot be denied, but you lose the esteem of others when conceit enters your heart; vanity in your greatest merit will cause you to fall from nobility with the greatest disgrace. Praise in one's own mouth is the most certain vituperation!

It is always those who talk about themselves the least who gain the most esteem. The eagle does not show its royal feathers but receives the most applause for its majesty. And the phoenix herself, the only astonishment in the world, abhors vulgar ostentation; she is more anticipated and esteemed after her death than during her resurrection.

Even worse is sowing envy, which is vile, even more so in small hearts, which are easily filled with everything. Envy is sticky; it always finds something to grab, even from what is imagined. It is a cruel beast that, with the good of others, does so much harm to its own owner. Envy feeds on the entrails of its host, and the longer it feeds, the greater it torments, seeking to banish all humanity from him. It moves with cunning, seeded in jealousy and malice, declaring itself against others and seeking to destroy all that it does not possess. "Because if we achieve this," envy says, "then they cannot make that odious display of what they own. We will eclipse their bountifulness in this way: by destroying what they have, so that they have less than us!"

Now, what is not seen is as if it were not. And as that old satirist said, "Your knowledge is nothing if others do not know that you know." Things usually do not pass for what they are but for what they seem. There are many more fools than knowledgeable people. But because they dress in garments of guile, their appearance pays, and, although they have no substance, deception prevails and things are estimated from the outside.

The ostentatious are always loathed, and the more they expose themselves, the more foolish they look, because excellence depends more on luck and circumstances, than on time and nature. They cause the ailments of envy, which infect everything, turning applause into grievances and enraging vulgarity. Greatness and gallantry are bewitching, but when ostentatious, they transform everyone around them into a Basilisk[40], with a gaze that kills.

Therefore, distinguish yourself starting today, and look at your own decorum! If you have any brains, you will notice that when you most want to envy the abundance of others and when you want to dress yourself in garments of deception in order to fit in, it is then that you discover the greatness of your ugliness, seated in your extremities.

Ostentation is always vulgar and destined to fade. She causes aversion in others and is discredited among the sane. The gallant retreat, the prudent minimize, and the discreet embrace modesty, and they all live safely, contenting themselves with satisfying themselves. They do not pay for themselves through deceptive appearances, nor do they sell them. Reality is enough; they do not need extrinsic and contrived applause. In a word, you are the symbol of riches; it is not sanity but danger to publicize yourself.

But what good is reality without appearance? The greatest wisdom is knowing how to showcase wisdom. Knowing is twofold: knowing and knowing how to display what you know. I would say about showcasing what others say about luck: that an ounce of it is worth more than riches without it.

----
40   A basilisk, in European legend, is a serpent king who causes death to anyone who looks at him.

What is the benefit of being relevant if its relevance is not readily apparent? If the sun did not dawn, making a most lucid display of its rays; if the rose, among the flowers, were always imprisoned in its bud and did not display its fragrant wheel of petals; if the diamond, aided by art, did not change its backgrounds, highlights, and reflections; what use would so much light, so much aroma, and so much value be if their extravagance did not enhance them? I am the rays of sunlight; I am the rose petal; I am the jewel of nature, and since heaven gave me perfection, I must use discernment in how I display my extravagance.

The first thing to which the God of all creation attended was the display of all things he would later create, for he first raised the light and with it the means of shining. He was, and remains, truly worthy of the first applause. Since light reveals everything else, the maker himself created it first. This is proof that it is just as important to know how to showcase as it is to showcase. Discernment in how you show the extravagance of your genius should be rooted in divinity and decorum.

Astute discernment asks which matters more: reality or appearance? There are things that seem very big in themselves yet are very small in reality, and, conversely, there are others that seem small yet, in reality, are very big, like an ordinary monstrosity. Such are the consequences of ostentation, or a lack thereof. Side with prudence when you showcase the fullness of supplies and material things, and in how you display your home, its adornments, and your entourage.

However, the virtues of the mind, which are purity of taste, clarity of thought, maturity in judgment, and, when the season calls for it, firmness of will, are good to always showcase. On the day you master all four, you will be made triumphant, especially if you are in the presence of nobility and other men of influence.

There are anomalous people for whom a little looks like a lot, yet even they admire the men of discernment and decorum who, when possessing eminence as well, form a prodigy. And on the contrary, we've seen eminent men who, because they lacked those enhancements, did not seem like half of a discrete man. So, being discerning and using good decorum in how you display the extravagance of your genius will give true shine to your heroic garments and serve as a second entity in everything you do.

But this is understood only when reality confirms it; without merit and virtue, it is nothing more than vulgar deception and affectation, serving only to please defects and obtain abhorrent contempt from people instead of applause.

Merit and virtue can only be attained through experience and gained with the passage of time. Yet some are in a great hurry to go out and show themselves in the universal theater, and what they end up doing is displaying their nothingness and ignorance; reality then denies them. In trying to display the extravagance of their upstanding nature, they foolishly proclaim their defects. And now, rather than being remembered for their splendor of merit and virtue, they forever live in the infamy of their mistakes and ignorance.

No enhancement asks to be less influenced than extravagance, as it can quickly turn into envy, a terminal ailment, and one that has caused so many to perish. This is because extravagance quickly causes contempt. Therefore, you must be very moderate with it and use it only on occasion. With it, temperance of the mind is even more necessary than that of the body; material life needs to be guided by moral life so that your errors are gilded by moderation.

Sometimes extravagance consists more in a mute eloquence, in showing eminence tactfully, perhaps in a prudent dissimulation, or in a plausible display of courage. Sometimes, hiding merits and virtues is better than announcing them, because silence on a matter of curiosity tends to sting humans very quickly, which can be used to your benefit.

Use, then, this art with happiness, and enhance it more with artifice! It is a great trick not to showcase yourself all at once but to navigate encounters with a compass, depicting your perfection a little at a time and always advancing it.

Let every enhancement be seen as an advancement, and let every enhancement be called greater than the previous one! And with the applause of one skill, new expectations for another will be aroused, so applause is always maintained and admiration always fed. The same is true for exploits.

But, coming to our point, I say, and I feel very strongly about this, that it would be an inconceivable act of violence to grant the fox his cleverness, the lion his strength, and the peacock his beauty, and then deny them the ability to boast about and display the extravagance of that which identifies them. Not even nature, in all its wisdom, would do this! Because to do so would be to condemn its own providence, and against the force of nature there are no precepts in which reason does not intervene. And even then, whatever fears the gallows may provoke, nature can revoke with its own power.

In his wisdom, the Holy Creator has also provided a remedy for unchecked extravagance and ostentation, should they one day empoison nature. It is as easy as it is effective, and it is this: that the fox, the lion, and the peacock be seriously commanded and criminally ordered, that every time they display the wonders of their natural endowments, they be reminded of their imperfections.[41] That the fox be reminded of his fragile physique every time he needs to showcase his cleverness. That the lion be reminded of his poor stamina whenever he displays his strength. And that the peacock be reminded of the ugliness of his feet every time he looks down to show the lavishness of his plumage. I assure you that this alone is enough to reform unchecked extravagance and ostentation, both with animals and with humanity!

Perfection belongs only to God.

----
41   The fox cannot stand and fight because he is fragile, and so he has to rely on his cunning to survive. The lion, although powerful, has poor stamina, and so he cannot exert his great strength for very long, and the peacock, although beautiful in plumage, has ugly feet, which he has to see whenever he wishes to showcase his feathers because he has to look down in order to do so. All of which serve as a reminder that only God is perfect, and our greatest strength also serves as our greatest weakness; thus, there is no room for conceit in God's economy.

-XIV-

A Man of Self-Possession

Invectives

Zeus resides on the king of mountains, Mt. Olympus, not because it towers over the tallest heights, an obligation of its superiority; not because its greatness is flaunted everywhere, an object of imitation; not because it is the first to receive the splendor of solar rays in the morning; not because it is crowned with stars, the apex of happiness; not because it names the heavens, a matter of fame and command; but because it never submits to the vulgar and strange impressions of nature! At most, the winds come to kiss its feet, the clouds become its carpet, and nothing goes beyond that. Mt. Olympus never flinches at nature, irrefutable proof of its impassioned eminence! The greatest dominion is that of oneself.

The Complete Man of great capacity does not surrender to the vulgar alterations of humor or to those of affection; he always remains superior to such intemperate material. This is the product of his prudence and the effect of his self-reflection, which allows him to recognize his eminent position as the Lord over his own mind.

In contrast, the debased, those men who are unworthy of lordship, are constantly tyrannized by the prevailing humor and ordinary vulgarity of the era; they mar their reputation and character with the foolishness they speak and the mistakes they make. They support today that which they contradicted yesterday. And although they may sometimes flirt with reason, they usually end up running her over with their poor decorum and intemperate behavior. Thus, they remain in a constant state of perennial judgment by their peers, which is the most absurd of stupidities.

Such people should not be taken into consideration because they lack the reason to make sound judgments. From today to tomorrow, they are contradictory—first contrary to themselves, then later they contradict everyone else. It is better then, knowing their incongruous nature, to leave them in their confusion. The more involved they become in a matter, the worse they make it.

They contradict everything and, in their idiocy, even go against nature, all without any facts or knowledge of the matters at hand. Not only does their incivility exhaust the will of those around them, but when challenged, they also dare to go to trial, certain they will not be found guilty of ignorance! Unchecked determination and a lack of self-awareness quickly turn into stubbornness and incompetence if not prevented.

It is very important to know and recognize this type of intemperate behavior in others in order to overcome it. And, even then, it would be in your best interests to decline to even engage them. If you ever doubt the averageness of a man, faithfully side with prudence.

Empathy argues to prevent this behavior or try to correct it, but this is a delusion of the mind. Know the prudent in order to choose them and the imprudent in order to flee from them. Never open the door to one evil, because many others lurk outside waiting for the chance to sneak in. A person swayed by emotions cannot speak of things as they are because they are ruled by emotions and not reason. Be careful that your sympathy for the recalcitrant and the pitiful does not ruin your reputation or make you unfortunate.

Then there are some men who are so extremely impertinent, who are always wisecracking, always limping with passion, intolerable to those who have to deal with them, stepfathers of conversation and enemies of affability, that they spoil every moment of good taste. They are, ordinarily, great opponents of all that is good and fathers of all foolishness. For every word of praise they utter, they give criticism as well, and for every point of agreement they concede, they have a point of contention. They oppose what others do simply because it was done without them. These types are easy to find but difficult to get along with. Everything rubs them the wrong way, and they contradict as many people as they encounter.

Undoubtedly, they are more irremediable than true madmen, because the latter might be worth entertaining, since in madness there may be some genius, but with the former, there is no use; since they lack reason, they cannot reason, and therefore, they cannot submit to reason. Where there is no sense, there is no feeling; the land of discontentment is spacious and filled with these monsters.

Whoever has not experienced these people should note that there are entire nations affected by their ailment. Study the principles of these exotic monstrosities, but exercise courage and caution in probing them. It's better to see the study of them as a hilarious sport, so you can protect your sanity, or your gallantry may be short-lived.

But when two of the same ill-tempered insolents get involved with each other, let the Complete Man, master of discernment, look but not intervene. It will guarantee him the best time, as long as he is secure and looking on from the fence of his sanity at those two bulls of imbecility.

As for you, be sure that you rarely get angry, and if you do, may it be with plenty of occasion and never with any vulgarity. In truth, never experiencing indignation is not a reasonable expectation for humankind. But to always be cloaked in perennial rudeness and anger, and towards all sorts of people, is an intolerable effrontery. Also, the distaste caused by another's naiveté must not become an opening for your anger. Whoever does not have the capacity to know himself will not have the capacity to know others and make amends.

Guard yourself from men of absurdity who bathe themselves in contradiction. They hunt for opportunities they can fill with contention and raise arguments against because they are insufferable harpies, enemies of good taste who lacerate everything with their actions and upset everyone with their words.

And should their fiery personality be mistakenly welcomed by someone naive and unwise, but with good intentions, they will quickly overstay their welcome, progressing from presumptuous to malicious, before finally becoming a monster of impertinence.

-XV-

Discernment and Immediacy
Problems

Once upon a time, lightning was the most certain weapon of the fabulous Zeus; in its instantaneous power, he found and achieved his greatest victories; with his thunderbolt, he quickly triumphed over rebellious giants. You see, satisfaction largely depends on immediacy, for alacrity is the mother of happiness. In life, the eagle instructs us because his enhancements of speed always come from the skies of ingenuity.

There are men of excellence in thought and men of excellence in extreme immediacy. The former causes admiration and the latter satisfaction; find these men and emulate them.

"Quick enough is good enough," says the old adage. But the problem with this perspective is that we never examine promptness or delay, but rather the perfection of outcome; this is how our esteem for things is governed. There are those accidents that are ignored or forgotten because their success remains.

What is quickly done will be quickly undone. What takes an eternity to do will take another eternity to undo. And what has to last an eternity must take another to be done. The more tender your children are, the more easily the evil one will swallow them up.

But if all success is due esteem, then to sudden success, applause, and cheers; for that success now doubles in eminence, thanks to its immediacy and the satisfying end it brings to the human experience of impatience.

Some people think a lot, yet still fumble everything later, while others get everything right without thinking beforehand. The vivacity of wit and intuition will always supplement the depths of judgment and prevent the need for consultation.

Wit and intuition are gifts from providence; there is no substitution for them. Guard yourself against the quick flattery of good taste and the immediate charm of admiration, for they sometimes make the fallacious seem so plausible, lest your superlatives fail to prevent unthinkable mediocrities from coming out.

He who falls in love with patience and entrusts himself to time allies himself with victory: guidance, providence, reasoning, maturity, waiting—they all guarantee success, but they all require time. In contrast, entrusting yourself to suddenness means only entrusting yourself to speed and luck.

As Solomon reminds us, "There is a time for everything."[42] The guidance of providence will be mapped in your discernment and intuition, so you will know the way.

When providence prevents, prudence disposes, and reason assists, the execution of action should be aborted. Here, promptitude and courage will bring success and give birth

----
42   See Ecclesiastes 3.

to a favorable outcome! Champion the success of decisiveness in view of the error of reconsideration. Knowing when to stop or change course is more important than knowing when to start... The will of God is immovable.

Some attribute these successes to fortune alone, but they are also due to a prodigious perspicacity. This type of heroic enhancement is an art that brings bliss and is a blessing from nature. There is no trickery or artifice that can buy you time in moments of extremity. Therefore, arm yourself beforehand by mastering composure, to protect yourself against suffocation, and discernment, to protect yourself against confusion. Difficulty is a woman who cannot make up her mind. Sometimes she arrives, and sometimes she does not. Sometimes she is easy to deal with, and other times she is complicated. With her, you will sometimes see and then overcome, and other times you will overcome and then see.

Therefore, it is imperative that one tests his spirit in the tightest of circumstances and his intelligence against works of opposition. Harsh predicaments should be used to increase the value of insight and the endurance of judgment. The greater the bind, the greater the insight, the greater the urgency, the greater the discernment, and the greater the risk, the greater one's mental performance. Thus, one should always look for opportunities that strengthen his fortitude and exercise his genius and ingenuity, while always wearing the gloves of prudence.

It is true that there are anomalous situations that may cause one to suddenly get everything right in action even while getting everything incorrect in thought: unexpected and unexplained occurrences of fortune. These situations usually do not offer later what they offer at the present moment. When one's discernment recognizes these situations, there is no need to wait for reconsideration or to appeal at a later time. One should immerse himself in them, with eminent promptitude and with faith in the coming rewards that providence has provided for him in them; do not fear contingencies.

Showing great discernment in moments of great immediacy brings great admiration. One such moment was enough to accredit Solomon with being the greatest sage to ever live, making him more venerated than all of his wealth and power ever could.[43]

Two others, Alexander the Great[44] and Emperor Julius Caesar[45], both of whom deserved to be the firstborns of fame, also had such a moment.

The former experienced his when he cut the insoluble knot with his sword, proving himself worthy of being ruler of Asia. And the latter cemented himself in history when he faced his own impossible knot: staying in Gaul or crossing the river.[46] For both champions, these moments of great immediacy called for great discernment. They were the ultimate test of providence, sent to measure their worth as men and whether they were capable of commanding the world.

----

43   The Judgement of Solomon, as recounted in 1 Kings 3:16-28.

44   Alexander the Great and the insoluble knot: It had been prophesied that the one who could untie the impossible knot would become the ruler of Asia. But instead of trying to untie the impossibly difficult knot, Alexander just cut through it with his sword. He went on to conquer Asian kingdoms as far east as Afghanistan.

45   Julius Caesar was forced to choose between living in enmity with Rome as the ruler of Gaul or crossing the Rubicon River, invading Rome, and becoming Emperor of the entire Roman Empire if victorious.

46   In both examples, their difficult decisions are labeled as a type of "Gordian Knot" by Gracián—an intricate problem or an insoluble one.

When quick wit is confirmed by acumen, acclaim is garnered. When alacrity results in a favorable effect, it argues for eminence in the cause.

Perfection attained at the end overshadows any difficulty experienced in the beginning. All the more estimable if it goes from acute to prudent and from wit to acumen.

The jewels of discernment and immediacy adorn the greatest heroes, accrediting them with the deepest depths and arming them with the highest capacity of perspicacious acumen. With them on, heroes are often recognized with admiration and pondered with applause. Such is the case with our great Spanish hero Don Francisco María Carrafa, the Most Excellent Duke of Nochera, whose prodigious display of these jewels during times of bold and daring exploits cut through the thread of luck, his eminent brilliance becoming more luminous the more difficulty he encountered. These jewels are a gift from providence, and they are not beholden to anything, not even fortune. He faced the most desperate of situations with the utmost lordship, imperturbability of mind, clarity of thought, and firmness of will, bringing others relief through his promptness and execution of sound judgment. When others shrugged in doubt, he stood tall with confidence. There was nothing that escaped his attention or confused his vivacity; he was the perfect emulation of genius and ingenuity.

And although he lacked happiness at the end of his life, he did not lack fame.

This is usually the case with heroes.[47]

In generals and champions, possessing these qualities is the greatest advantage, as compelling as it is sublime, because it makes almost all their actions sudden and their executions swift; contingencies cannot be studied nor prevented from being a matter of chance. You have to act on the occasion, which consists of the triumph of your acumen and the success of your promptness over any given situation; your victories depend on this.

In kings, contemplation and pensiveness are better because all of their actions are eternal. They think for many and use prudence as an auxiliary, and everything is necessary for universal success. They are rulers of time and have a bed where resolutions can mature, thinking through entire nights to get the days right. Kings exercise their heads more than their hands.

----

47   Don Francesco María Carrafa was Duke of Nochera and Captain General of the Kingdoms of Aragon and Navarre. From a noble Neapolitan family, he pursued a military career in the cavalry of the Spanish army and was field master of the Piedmont and Monferrato regions.

In 1639, when conflict with Catalonia broke out, he asked King Philip IV to act prudently to prevent the Catalans from surrendering to France. Baltasar Gracián served him as adviser, priest, and confessor when they both went to deal with the Catalonian problem. Both he and Gracián sided with moderation, equidistant between the repressive measures of the Crown and the Catalonian demands. But his mediation was rejected, and due to his opposition to the policy followed by Gaspar de Guzmán, the Count of Olivares, he was imprisoned in the Torre de Pinto jail and charged with collaborating with the French.

He died on July 12, 1642, after a long legal process. Around those years, Gracián published his second book, El Politico, and dedicated it to the duke. The title page reads: "To His Excellency, Don Francisco María Carrafa, the Duke of Nochera and Captain General in the Kingdoms of Aragon and Navarre."

-XVI-

Against Imposterism

Satirical

Only fools laugh at the warnings and notes of observation of wisemen who have experience with both the divine and the cunning. These men know and recognize proper comportment, in others and especially in themselves.

The great cynic philosopher believed virtue revealed in action was better than virtue revealed in theory. He used his simple lifestyle and behavior to criticize the social values and institutions of what he saw as a corrupt, imposterous, and feigned society. Diogenes[48], with his burning torch at noon, broke through a large crowd of reprobates gathered in the street. Examining everyone as he passed them by, he was stopped and asked, "What are you doing with a torch at noon?"

---

48   Diogenes the Cynic was a Greek philosopher and one of the founders of cynicism. He modeled himself on the example of Heracles, believing that virtue was better revealed in action than in theory. He became notorious for his philosophical stunts, such as carrying a lamp during the day and claiming to be "looking for an honest man." He criticized Plato, disputed his interpretation of Socrates, sabotaged his lectures, and distracted his listeners by bringing food and eating during his discussions. Diogenes was also noted for having mocked Alexander the Great, both in public and to his face, when he visited Corinth in 336 BC.

He replied, "I am looking for men. I will settle for one, but I can't find any."

"Well, what about all of these?" they replied. "Aren't they men?"

"No!" answered the philosopher; "figures of men, yes… real men, no!"

Many believed him to be absolutely crazy, because dogs bark at what they cannot understand.

Garments that are garnished with the jewels of plausibility, that of what "seems to be," once examined for authenticity, are revealed to be covered in salient defects. These receive very little grace from contemporaries and suffer the universal contempt of all. They instantly become notorious and infamous for being counterfeit, and so the relationship between these garments and impropriety is forever seen as analogous to everything that is of fraud and forgery. As it is with these garments, so it is with people.

There are many landlords of imposterism and those who want to be affected by them. Who, in order to differentiate themselves from other men, follow an extravagant and often immoderate singularity and observe it in everything. Oh, Lord, I would prefer to speak like a dead man or, better yet, look like one than to speak with a mouth like theirs and look as ridiculous as they do. They transform their voice, affect it with tone, invent languages and dialects, concoct grievances, and embarrass themselves with their behavior. Above all, they torture good taste, driving decorum out of its mind. They have more in common with brutes than with other men. And, when confronted about their improprieties, they deny them with singular violence—more an admission of their level of ignorance than a show of strength. This incomprehension extends past their behavior and quickly affects their decision-making. Too dumb to even know what is good for them, they drink bleach and celebrate it as nectar, trade the liqueurs of a generous king for the syrup of the commoner, and eat the brown bread of peasants rather than baptize their stomachs with the ambrosia of the gods. There is also a coldness to them, and they lack generosity, an indictment of their spiritual bankruptcy.

Consequently, they invent things every day to carry out their extravagances, and they do a good job of it because the common man, with no discernment, cannot differentiate between what is real and what is false in the things they exaggerate. However, the Complete Man does not fancy them and leaves them with their extravagance—or what he calls impertinence.

In this way, he always behaves. In every circumstance he encounters where they attempt to normalize their display of extravagance and taste, they are repudiated by his level headedness, no matter how much they try to deceive him. He knows them well, and he remains unmoved when others shower them with praise. He is like a wine expert who, upon viewing a novice unable to contain himself while drinking from an outdated bottle of wine, exclaims: "O most precious nectar, you only pretend to conquer the taste of balsam[49] and the sweetness of alchermes![50] It is pitiful that you are so vulgar in reality; you would be the idol of

----

49   Balsam is a traditional Eastern and Northeastern European herbal, high alcohol content (40-45%) liqueur, originally used for medicinal purposes.

50   Alchermes is a classic Italian liqueur, full-bodied, rich in spicy aromas and with hints of citrus. It has been used for centuries for the preparation of homemade desserts.

wise men if they didn't know any better. You can only fool the inexperienced."

The well-known thing is that some men run to imitate the vulgar vices of the most vile of men and of brutes themselves, and then in human affairs they want to dictate sanctity.

In heroic actions, singularity is best; few are the things that inspire more veneration than gallantry in a deed. In the highness of the spirit and in high thoughts dwells greatness. There is no nobility like that of the heart which never descends into vileness. It is the virtue character of heroism, and it displays the differences between the Complete Man and the secular man very clearly.

A prince must dwell with such brilliance of qualities and with such splendor of virtues that if the stars of heaven left their celestial spheres and came down to dwell among us, they would live in no other way than in emulation of him.

What benefit is the fragrance of amber if the stench of one's behavior overpowers it? It may well embalm the body, but it cannot immortalize the soul. There is no scent like that of a good name, nor a fragrance like that of good fame, which is perceived from afar, comforts the attentive, and leaves a trace of applause for the theater of the world, that will last for centuries, long after one is gone.

But, just as affectation, which all sane people hiss at, makes some of them abhorrent and even intractable, it makes others unique by fueling their desire not to be like them or even appear similar. This means living practically, accommodating the ordinary, and marrying the serious with the human experience—things well exemplified by His Excellency, The Count of Aguilar and Marquis of La

Hinojosa[51], our second patron. He was so endearing and so loved by everyone that even his enemies applauded his life and mourned his death. I heard many, and very sane people say about him: "He really knew how to be a lord and the definition of authenticity!" … words worthy of such a great hero.

There is another kind of male who is in no way a man and is even worse than an imposter, and if the former is vexatious, then the latter is ridiculous; it is those, I say, who purposely differ in fashion and who, in their insanity, trade their reputation for attention, even if it is negative. They abhor the pragmatic and show antipathy towards society by doing so. They resurrect old fashions, which should become more celebrated with antiquity, only to make them look foolish with their behavior. There are those who in Spain dress like the French and in France like the Spanish. They might as well go to war wearing a golilla[52] or go to court wearing a matachin[53]. If they had any sense, they would pay attention to where they are and dress properly. The fisga[54] was not made for sausages!

Your behavior should never cause you to be the object of derision. There are many reasons people mock and ridicule, and you should not be one of them. Laughing matter is never to be given, not even to a child, and much less to sane and judicious males; yet there are many who seem to put all

----

51   **Juan de Mendoza y Velasco: The Count of Aguilar and Marquis of la Hinojosa. He held the following positions: Marquis de la Hinojosa, Governor of Milan, Viceroy of Navarre, and Knight of the Military Order of Santiago. He is considered one of King Philip III's most important ministers.**

52   **A golilla is a starched white collar worn by Spanish magistrates.**

53   **A matacin is a uniform worn by carnival dancers in 17th century Spain.**

54   **A fisga is a trident harpoon used for catching large fish.**

of their attention into only making people laugh and who only study how to entertain the gossipy. And when they do not come out with something ridiculously unique, their day is wasted, and they are seen as useless. There are some vices that are matters of others: ingratitude is a matter of envy; discontentment is a matter of covetousness; and in this particular case, foolishness, the pasture of murmuring.

And if frivolous singularity, the offspring of indiscretion, causes great visible irritation, imagine how much more it must irritate the inside, and by that I mean the soul? There are some who seem to have been fitted by nature with taste and wit that are in reverse, and they affect it by not following what is customary. But these are exceptions to the rule. Exotic in flow, paradoxical in taste, and anomalous in everything, they undoubtedly turn those who claim to understand them into the greatest imposters.

Others put their whims at the mercy of their vanity, which, when their ego is bruised, leads to sudden swellings of rage born of crazy fantasies and lined with foolishness; their ego is easily hurt, and so this happens often with them. Thus, they have an angry seriousness about everything and towards everyone. You cannot take these types seriously or take their affronts personally. It's better to have a kind of pitiful mercy on them and laugh with indifference.

There are too many people and even entire nations plagued by this "humor," and if laughter is not the remedy for one of these singularities of pique, then what would work for such a ridiculous multitude of them? If dealing with one is exhaustive, imagine dealing with many! Shrug them all off with a cold shoulder and remain indifferent.

Let it be that you speak with wisdom, act with decorum, are serious about custom, and embrace heroic actions! This makes the Complete Man venerated and leaves no room for presumptions. May this critical discourse also remind you of the seriousness and importance of speech, which always adheres to decorum! Never skimp on preserving the flower of respect, and protect your esteem with mindful behavior, just as you would protect yourself and others from the blade of your sword by keeping it in its sheath. May it condemn any excess of vain singularities, which all end up as useless affectations.

Is there a remedy that would be so effective that it would cure all of them of being imitators of impropriety and return them to being men? Well, there really is, and it's infallible. I leave sanity, which is the common remedy for all ills, and go to the most singular of singularities. The remedy for this illness is to look at another who is similarly affected: someone extravagant, imposterous, shameless, and impertinent. To look at him is to look at oneself in a mirror of errors and to notice the laughter that his behavior causes in others, to ponder its ugliness and its ridiculousness, and to be affected by it, or, better put, to see oneself in him. This is sufficient to make one effectively abhor all kinds of imposterous behavior and even tremble at the slightest hint or mere thought of it.

XVII

The Maturity of a Man

Dialogue between
Dr. Don Manuel de Salinas y Lizana,
Canon of the Holy Church of Huesca,
and the author

AUTHOR: Remarkable singularity, that of the Persians, in not wanting to see their children until they were seven years old! Even paternal love, which is without a doubt the greatest, was not enough to deny, or at least conceal, the imperfections of common childhood. They did not count them as their children until they could reason for themselves.

CANON: Imagine! If a father cannot suffer an ignorant son and waits seven years for him to reason in order to establish a relationship and confabulate with him, it should not surprise us to see intelligent men unable to tolerate fools and dismiss them from the presence of their cultured genius.

AUTHOR: Nature, although so generous, does not lead her works to perfection the first day, and neither does the diligence of art; each day they advance, a little at a time, until they reach their fullness, and you give them their compliments.

CANON: This is why the beginnings of all things are small. This is even the case with very great things, where we see that, little by little, they reach perfection; every day, a little more is perfected. The things that quickly reach their perfection are worth little and last less; a flower is soon made and soon undone, but a diamond, which took time to form, appeals to eternity.

AUTHOR: Without a doubt, this same thing happens in men, who do not and cannot suddenly make themselves perfect. So they start with small things, each day perfecting themselves a little more at a natural pace, until they reach the fullness of the Complete Man: pure in taste, clear in thought, mature in judgment, and firm in will.

CANON: That is so true! Everyday we experience this when we meet people who are on their journey to this fullness but are not there yet, and you can tell they are not yet completely done because they lack something, and sometimes that something is the most important. The degree to which this varies depends on the subject you encounter. Some are at the very beginnings of genius, but they still have a lot to learn; others are more advanced in everything; and some have already reached the consummation and fullness of their gifts. It takes a lot to become a fully accomplished man.

AUTHOR: In this manner, I would say man is like a generous liquor that is good, and even more so, like a good wine. One that, when it begins to mature, has an ungrateful sweetness and an insubstantial rigidity to it, as it is not yet done. But as it begins to boil, it begins to separate itself from that primitive rawness that was so present, correcting that annoying sweetness and acquiring a very soft generosity. At this point, it flatters with its color and with the fragrance it solicits; it is then that it becomes a pasture for men and a delectable nectar.

So I understand why, to avoid any unpleasantries, Jupiter further nurtured his son Bacchus, sewing him to his knee, and securing for him the discreet palates of the brain, before introducing him.[55]

CANON: In this way, just like wine slowly maturing in a vessel, the mind is slowly maturing in the fragile vessel of the body, with reason, clarity, and even mood improving every day. All men have in them an angry sweetness from their childhood, an invasive crudeness about them: a taste for pleasures, an inclination to do little and less than serious things, youthful jobs, frivolous occupations; and although we perhaps may rarely get a hint of maturity, anticipating it is futile, because they are usually far from ready. This is something that should be cognitively attended to because it cannot be hidden, at least not for very long. Eventually, whether naturally or affectedly, you will slip into youthful slights and bouts of immaturity, and it will be implied that you are still not a complete man.

AUTHOR: Time is a great healer and revelator of truths because of his age and experience.

CANON: He alone can cure the improprieties of youth, which is a great aliment. In maturity, the thoughts are greater and more elevated; taste is more enhanced; wit is purified; judgment is seasoned; and will is ironed, and at last a complete man is made: a man that is refined, pleasant, and even

----

55   Bacchus, the Roman god of wine, is the son of the Roman god Jupiter and the Theban princess Semele. With Bacchus still in her womb, Semele was killed by flames upon seeing Jupiter in his divine form. Jupiter quickly sewed Bacchus into his knee and carried him to term, nurturing him until he was ready to be born, "to avoid any unpleasantries". (Jupiter, being male, does not have a womb, so he bounced Bacchus on his knee until he was full-term.) The interpretive meaning being that, just as wine tastes bitter and is unpleasant to swallow unless it is fully aged, the incomplete man is bitter and difficult to deal with until he fully matures.

appetizing to the company of connoisseurs. He comforts with his advice, warms with his efficiency, delights with his speech, and all of him smells of a very chivalrous generosity.

AUTHOR: But before they are seasoned, what harshness they give us in everything—what recalcitrance in understanding, what acidity in dealing, what discomfort in bearing!

CANON: What a torment it is for an already mature and sane man to have to adjust, either out of necessity or out of convenience, to one of these incomplete and insufferable people! A torment that even exceeds the one of Phalaris[56], when he tied a living person to a dead person, hand to hand and mouth to mouth.

AUTHOR: The Complete Man in his wisdom, goes over the ignorance and improprieties of his past. He recognizes the stains that were left by his imprudence, and he finds within himself the imperfections that caused said behavior, so that he may indict them and take them to trial. He then judiciously condemns those faults and emotions that led to those poor decisions.

CANON: The evil is that some men never fully mature.

AUTHOR: They are always missing a crucial part, and it's usually purity in taste (which is bad) or maturity in judgment (which is worse).

CANON: And many times we notice that they are missing something, but we do not succeed in defining what it is.

---

56 Phalaris was a Sicilian tyrant from the sixth century who was known for his cruelty. Here, the canon uses a euphemism to say that it would be a fate worse than torture or death for a refined and complete man to have to deal with an immature and incomplete man-child.

AUTHOR: I have also noticed that time is never even and brings men to maturity at different paces.

CANON: It's that for some Chronos[57] flies, and for others he limps; for some he is ready to use his wings, and for others he takes out his crutches. There are some who very quickly achieve perfection in any matter; there are others who take a long time to do it, and sometimes with universal harm, as when obligations are involved. Also, men not only need to grow in the common perfection of prudence but also in the particularities of each job and employment.

AUTHOR: And what about kings?

CANON: Yes, kings are born unmade, and this is an even greater matter of prudence and experience because a thousand perfections are necessary for them to reach their full majesty. Generals are only made at the cost of their own blood and the blood of others; orators, after much study and practice; and even doctors, who in order to raise one from a bed must throw a hundred into the grave. They are all being done until they reach the point of their perfection.

AUTHOR: And I ask: that point, which they reach, is it one that is fixed?

CANON: No, and that is the unhappiness of inconstancy. There is no constant happiness on earth because there is no fixed star, and so there is no constant state of rest. There is instead a continuous mutability in everything. Either it grows or it declines, always raving with so much variation.

----

57 **Chronos is the Greek god of time.**

AUTHOR: Our order, that of humanity, follows the natural order, and with age, our memory and even our understanding begin to fade.[58]

CANON: Yes! And for that reason, it is convenient to achieve things early in their season and to know how to enjoy things at their peak, even when they peak late, and especially how to enjoy much more knowledgeable men, who are filled with wisdom and experience.

AUTHOR: Much is required to climb the summit of maturity and reach the height of perfection and its jewels.

CANON: First Vulkan hammers, and then Numen contributes;[59] the favor of nature requires you to be cultured, studious, and in continuous dealings with wise men, even with those already dead, by way of their books; doing this brings them to life, and it is like having a conversation with their spirit. The favor of nature also requires faithfulness to experience, judicious observation, prudence in the handling of sublime matters, and in the variety of employment and skills. Careful attention to all of these things works to bring out a consummate man, a completely made and perfect man who knows himself, the correctness of his judgment,

----

58   Although Gracián did not know it at the time (it would be Rudolf Clausius, the German mathematician and physicist, who would discover it in the 1800s), he was describing the second law of thermodynamics, which states that all things trend from order to disorder.

59   Vulkan is the Roman god of fire, and Numen, in Roman mythology, is a divine spirit that presides over things. Here, the canon uses an allegory to say that, before God or nature blesses you with the virtues of a complete man, your imperfections and immaturities must be purified by fire, and then the more perfect version of you must be forged in that fire; in other words, you must go through hardship to be purified and then go through trials in order to be forged and shaped. An example of this is the process of making a great sword, which starts with the purification of an imperfect metal and ends with the blacksmith hammering the sword into perfect shape.

and the purity of his taste; he speaks attentively, acts with restraint, is wise in deed, is sane in deed, and is the center of all perfection.

AUTHOR: Now I say that there is not enough appreciation for The Complete Man!

CANON: There is no good achievement that I do not appreciate. We should look to him as a friend, win him over as a counselor, oblige him to be a protector, and beg him to be our teacher.

XVIII

A Man of Culture and Refinement

Heroic Fiction

Your father was Ingenuity, the Chiron[60] of nature; you were born from his care to be the perfection of everything; without you, the greatest actions go to waste and the best deeds lose their radiance. We have seen prodigious men, both incredibly intelligent and inventive, attempt to journey without you, only to walk in a manner so unrefined and inelegant that they reaped contempt rather than applause.

The most serious and learned sermon was dismayed without your grace; the most authoritative claim, useless without your priming; the most erudite book, ignored without your adornment; and, at last, we have seen the rarest inventiveness, the wisest choice, the deepest erudition, and even the sweetest eloquence, without your sophisticated enhancements, be accused of being nothing more than an unworthy vulgar barbarity and condemned to oblivion.

On the contrary, we see others that, when examined rigorously, have no known eminence, ingenuity, or depth, and yet they are plausible and praised solely for their finesse and

----

60   Chiron, the wisest of all centaurs, was the teacher of the Greek heroes Jason, Hercules, Asklepios, and Achilles. He was well versed in medicine, music, prophecy, and hunting, having been raised and educated by Apollo and his wife, Artemis.

orderliness. Perfection, or lack thereof, is transcendental and affects every other gift.

Now, a note about perfection: what is ugly often overcomes beauty because perfection tends to grow overconfident, and overconfidence always leads to defeat. History is full of examples of talented people who relished their own perfection, and these overconfident ones were always vanquished. The greater the talent, the more noticeable its lackluster points are; talent on its own seems to naturally draw the attention of envy to its inelegance and crudeness. So with perfection, remember, a little seems like a lot, and without it, a lot seems like nothing.

You had for your mother Good Disposition, the one that gives each thing its proper place, the one that brings harmony to everything. Everything and everyone in life has a proper place; outside of that place, everything naturally suffers violence, becomes artificial, and is thrown into confusion. The same seating in the sky for one star may result in its exaltation and for another its detriment, and so the brilliance of a star depends on where it is placed.

Disorder causes confusion, and what is careless and messy voids even the most sublime inventions. What is not composed or orderly is nothing more than a very crude, indigestible burden, a disgust to all good taste; things well composed not only bring joy with their release but also delight with their concert.

Discernment in choice would be sadly frustrated if careless men were to ruin it afterwards, and it is a pity that what it deserves for being excellent and select could be lost to uneducated barbarians. The sublime invention of the concepts, the subtlety in the speeches, and the studiousness in the various and select eruditions would all be in vain if a crude sloppiness and disorder came upon them afterwards. Do not ruin your talents, work, and reputation by lacking culture and refinement.

The creation displays the order and carefulness of the Almighty, who put everything in its proper place. When humans follow this example, sanctity follows suit, creating neatness and orderliness, which in turn edifies twice as much when it is twinned with a religious refinement. That great patriarch, the Archbishop of Valencia, Don Juan de Ribera[61], knew how to put both of these things together; he was as graceful as he was holy! And he even eternalized his piety and his culture in a lavish sacred college, where he inculcated in his learned and exemplary priests and ministers punctuality in rites, richness in ornaments, harmony in voices, devotion in worship, and refinement in everything.

Holiness does not gain from rudeness, nor does it lose from understanding. Today we see its sanctity in another patriarch, the illustrious Mr. Don Alonso Pérez de Guzmán[62], in whom virtue and discretion reside. Take note of this, because virtue is always seen, acknowledged, and admired; it makes a man so cultured, so perfect, and so seasoned. Your understanding must be pure, and your will must be well ordered. Let these two superpowers be refined; let your thoughts and your knowledge be neat and well polished, so

----

61   Juan de Ribera was an influential figure in 17th century Spain. He held appointments as Archbishop and Viceroy of Valencia, Latin Patriarchate of Antioch, President of the Audiencia, and Chancellor of the University of Valencia. He was beatified in 1796 and canonized by Pope John XXIII in 1960.

62   Alonso Pérez de Guzmán was a Spanish noble and hero of medieval Spain. He took command of the town and castle of Tarifa in order to defend them against the Moorish invasion after they had been secured by King Sancho IV. He is considered the founder of the line from which the Dukes of Medina Sidonia descend.

you will not be barbaric and disgraceful. Not only must the mind be cleaned, but the will as well. Let the operations of these two be pure and cultured, and let knowledge be seasoned, so you will not desire what is barbaric and rude!

Your brothers are Cleanliness, Good Taste, and Decorum, who beautify and season everything, not only on the outside of a man but much more in his inner attire, which are the garments of the true trappings of a person.

How uneducated and disheveled and how common was barbarity in the whole world before cultured Greece began to introduce refinement as it spread its empire! They made their cities cultured, both in the material of the buildings and in the formality of their citizens. They regarded other nations as barbarians, and rightfully so. They invented the three orders of architecture for the adornment of their temples and palaces, and the sciences for their famous universities. They knew how to be men because they were cultured and dressed in decorum.

And the Romans, with the greatness of their spirit and power, as they expanded their monarchy, extended their culture; not only did they emulate the Greeks, but they surpassed them, banishing the barbarity of almost everyone and making the world cultured and orderly in every way. There are still vestiges of that greatness and culture in some buildings, and when ordinary people ponder that greatness, they always call it *"la obra de los Romanos,"* the work of the Romans. This same culture and greatness can be traced on some statues that, owing to the rare skill of their craftsmen, perpetuate the fame of the heroes they represent. Even on the coins and stamps, this is visible and still admired, for they expected beauty in everything and showed intolerance for what was ugly.

There is a famous museum and theater of all that is ancient Greek and Roman, both in culture and refinement, in statues, stones, seals, coins, glasses, urns, plates, and jewelry, and it is all on display in our greatest friend, the cult and scholar Don Vincencio Juan de Lastanosa, who brings honor to the Romans with his refinement and glory to the Greeks with his ingenuity! Whoever wants to achieve all of this greatness together should frequent this original museum and theater and admire this learned and rare scholar of antiquity. He is a valuable Spanish coin, truly great in matter and rarity.

Where Roman culture and decorum are most extreme is in the immortal works of its prodigious writers. There it shines a light on the creativity of its writers and the feats of its warriors, eternally venerating the spirit of courage of some and the ingenuities of others.

Some former territories of the Roman Empire still preserve the wonder of this inherited aesthetic, especially cultured Italy, which stood as the center of that empire, with all of its cities aligned with beauty. But not all people and countries are worthy of mirroring. Here in Spain, curiosity reigns, and people care more about being eclectic than the beauty of their words, deeds, and aesthetics. They trade the long-lasting praise of a good reputation for the immediate attention their bizarre behavior garners. Even in France, the culture is so outlandish that it is strange, and this is even the case within the nobility. Therefore, venerate only the great European empires and esteem their arts, mirroring the gallantry, courage, and discretion of their heroes, so that everything will be perfectly on point in your comportment and you will radiate excellence everywhere you go.

Your children are called Advancement and Pleasure. In a garden, what flatters most, after the selection of plants and flowers, is their arrangement; how much more true is this in the garden of the spirit, where we admire the taste and fragrance of cultured men, their wise sayings, and the gallantry of their deeds, all of which are naturally enhanced by their eminence?

There are men who are naturally neat or orderly, in whom organization is a strength; they do not forgive the slightest disorder in their things; eminence is innate in them, both in their interior and exterior; they have a heart that is impatient with sloppiness. Alexander the Great affected the culture even through his armies, which, according to Quintus Curtius[63], seemed more like orderly senatorial compounds than lines of broken soldiers. Still, there are others with a heart so careless and disorganized that there is no room for order, compartmentalism, or even cleverness. Their lives are an exhibition of sloppiness and impatience, and thus everything that they work on shows crudeness and barbarism when examined under light.

It is said that the circumstances of a man greatly depend on the substance of that man. For substance is born of a natural ability, and in it is the composing fire of an iron will, polished action, and acquired wisdom. There is no greater example of this than Taicosama[64], who rose from being a servant to a powerful lord in Japan, becoming its master and great unifier; prodigious fortune with her seasoned hands worked a miracle, but only because he had given her a cultured, refined, and polished man to work a miracle for first!

----

63   Quintus Curtius was a Roman historian and author of the book *A History of Alexander the Great (42 A.D.).*
64   Toyotomi Hideyoshi (Japanese: 豊臣 秀吉) was a 16th century Japanese samurai and powerful lord of the late Sengoku period. He rose from a peasant background to become the most powerful man in Japan after unifying the country and becoming its *de facto* leader. He is regarded as the "Great Unifier" of Japan.

But the greatest enhancement of the Complete Man has to be how he affects others, and this is exemplified in the radiance and splendor of their faces when they see him. What is the point of being venerated and loved amongst people if they do not display those feelings for you?

In this way, the Three Graces[65] blessed His Excellency, Mr. Duarte Fernando Alvarez de Toledo[66], Grandee of Spain and Count of Oropesa. They assured him that everything in his constitution was copied from the cultured, the gallant, the courteous, the lucid, the practical, and from all that is erudite and discreet.

----

65   The Three Graces refers to the three goddesses in Greek mythology (Euphrosyne, Aglaia, and Thalia), from whom perfection was defined. Sometimes referred to as the Charites, they were the three goddesses of charm, beauty, nature, human creativity, goodwill, and fertility.

66   Duarte Fernando Alvarez de Toledo was a Spanish noble, military man, and statesman. He was Grandee of Spain, Count of Oropesa, Count of Deleytosa, Knight of the Order of Alcántara, Viceroy of Navarre, Valencia, and Sardinia, President of the Council of Orders and of the Council of Italy, and Ambassador in Rome.

XIX

A Man of Sound Judgment and Observation

Apologue

The very vulgar Momus[67], god of criticism and mockery, was constantly angry that he could not better observe the feelings of mortals, and so he called for a window into the human heart. He was censored and exiled from the company of the gods for this, and then further disillusioned upon learning that there are divinators of hearts who do not even need cracks to penetrate the most reserved interior. The transparent stained-glass window is pointless for those who look through long-sighted glasses. Knowing your own mind is the master key to unlocking another's heart.

The man of sound judgment and observation can become lord over any subject or object, an eagle of attention, and a lynx of understanding. He attentively probes the depths of the greatest mind, cautiously registers the sinuses of those hearts most bent on concealment, and judiciously measures the capacity of those around him. The sacredness of

----

67   Momus is the Greek god of blame, censure, and criticism. An evil-spirited god of blame and mockery, he brought negative feelings of failure, insignificance, and worthlessness to mortals. Representing the destructive force of fault-finding, he drained mortals of their confidence and found fault with them, as there was no way of looking into a human's heart to discern their true thoughts and intentions. Eventually, he was exiled from Mt. Olympus by Zeus.

his silence flushes out foolishness, and he discerns hypocrisy with the maturity of his judgment. He discovers, notices, warns, reaches, and understands everything, defining each thing by its essence.

Every great man is wise, just as every wise man is great. But these enhancements of superiority and understanding are reserved only for the highest of minds. It is good to be knowledgeable, but this is not enough; it is also necessary to be judicious! An eminent critic must first be excellent himself and then, from his perfection, rightly assign value to everything. He grades objects and subjects; he does not admire or despise everything, but from his eminence and high esteem, he assigns value to everything.

He then distinguishes between reality and appearance, for the Complete Man takes command of objects before they take hold of his intelligence or try to penetrate his emotions. He is a diviner and a master of intuition who understands how to look inside of things and not stop at the surface, who is not satisfied with the exterior, who does not pay attention to all that glitters. And so he utilizes his intellect in order to contrast and distinguish between what is false and what is true.

He is a great decipher of intentions and end results, who always carries a judicious counter-encryption with him. Deceit can boast of very few victories over him, and ignorance even fewer.

These eminences made Tacitus[68] a master of individuals and Seneca[69] a master of all mankind. There are no jewels more diametrically opposed to vulgarity than these: sound judgment and observation; they alone are enough to certify one as a wise man. He is cautious around common people who always tend to be malicious rather than judicious, who say everything but do not understand everything, and who seldom discern between what is real and what merely appears to be. Ignorance is very common, and it very commonly leads to errors. The Complete Man never bites at the bark and never feels disgust, since he never swallows deceit.

What a wonderful sight it is to see one of these deciphers of intentions and revelators of truth as he gains ground on these commoners of ignorance. Imagine if, reciprocally, two of these wise men, each with equal weapons of attention and intuition, and each wishing to reach the capacity of the other, were to duel for sport! With what dexterity they would undertake this challenge! What precision in their attacks! Oh, the attention to reason! What a test of their mental acuity! They would estimate each other's spirit, probe their affections, and weigh one another's prudence. They would not be satisfied with one or two successes, which could have been luck, or with two witty remarks, which could have easily been memorized.

In this way, the Complete Man must chart the anatomy of another's mind, examine its flow, registering and weighing both its speeches and affections, and from this high ground, use his excellence and superior capacity to decipher the subject matter in front of him. Like an eagle who examines its

---

68   Publius Cornelius Tacitus was a Roman historian and politician. He is regarded by modern scholars as one of the greatest Roman historians.

69   Lucius Annaeus Seneca was a Roman philosopher, stoic, statesman, and satirist.

prey before attacking, he takes inventory of a subject's entire anatomy, from head to heart, defining it in seconds and correctly estimating it according to the essence of its properties.

It is a great pleasure to meet one of these masters of men, who only in the faith of friendship expresses his feelings. These masters are prompt to censure others but slow to criticize them publicly. They also invoke one of the best strategies and greatest tricks for navigating life and publicity: thinking with the few and speaking with the many. But when, confident in a friendship and behind the back of trust, they vent their concepts, observations, and wisdom, oh, what they teach! Oh, what they illuminate! They place each person in the correct category, find the hidden meanings of each action, weigh each fact, shower each maxim with adulation, and disinfect each lie with the sunlight of their keen perceptions. Admire in them their extravagant objections to what others have been conditioned to believe as truth, and their deep observations, their subtle notes, their judicious tactics, their brave conceptions, their prudent thinking, and how much occurs to them and how little escapes their notice.

The most confident kings tremble before him and depose their own satisfactions in favor of his, for his judgments are an impeccable example of refinement.

He is intimate with the rigors of correct judgment, having proven himself through crucibles designed to bring out his finesse, and, as a result of this, the jewels produced within him are met with approval, and their contrast can pass and shine anywhere. They make him highly qualified, more so than with just the fickle crowd of commoners, whose vulgar estimations are not safe, for they tend to be more noise than discernment.

The things they idolize are often unable to survive scrutiny; and because they do not rely on a foundation of substantial integrity, their reputations are often worth little and are quickly cast aside. And so, a yes or no answer from one of these valiant judges, these masters of men, is worth more than all the acclaim of the secular world. It was not without cause that Plato called Aristotle his "entire school" and Antigonus spoke of Zeno as "the entire theater of my fame."[70]

The gifts of judgment and observation enhance every other gift found in their sphere: comprehension, knowledge, keenness, and the profound; and if they enhance some, they condemn others, such as gullibility, strange conceptions, and capriciousness, making certain that everything must be correct and complete.

But note that censure is very different from murmuring because the former speaks to indifference while the latter establishes malice. Just as a staunch censure celebrates the good, so too does it condemn the bad, all with equity and indifference.

This aphorism does not order the Complete Man to be malicious and cynical but rather intelligent and observant; he does not condemn everything, for that would be an abhorrent display of a lack of temper, nor does he applaud everything, for that would make his judgment worthless, for value is usually found in scarcity. There are some who only see the bad in anything and pick out the negatives from a multitude of positives; they conceive like vipers and burst

----
70   Aristotle was Plato's most famous student, and King Antigonus of Macedonia was an admirer and follower of Zeno, the founder of Stoicism. Here, Gracián says that the opinion of the Complete Man should be valued over that of secular men in the same way that Plato valued Aristotle more than all of his other students and King Antigonus credited Zeno as being the reason for his fame.

forth to spread their venom. In the end, these types are usually punished for the cruelty of their wits by being ostracized from society. It is one thing to be a distasteful momo, who feeds on what is rotten, and another to be an upright Cato, a lover of fairness and a model of integrity.

The Complete Man is like a judicious oracle of the truth, a passionate judge of merits, but he keeps to himself and only rubs shoulders with other wise men because the truth cannot be trusted to malice nor to ignorance: the former is guilty of evil, and the latter is guilty of incompetence. But when two or more of these masters of men meet, what great happiness is it when they communicate their feelings, crises, speeches, and knowledge; mark that moment with a precious stone and dedicate it to the Muses, to the Graces, and to Minerva.[71]

This kind of genius and ingenuity is not only good for speculating but is also very practical, especially for those in command, because, in its light, they discover the talents of their subjects, probe their capacities for distribution, measure their strengths and weaknesses, weigh their merits for just awards, and take the pulse of their character and fortitude. Genius and Ingenuity strike some from afar and others up close and personal; the latter will have everything because they are able to understand everything.

They choose with art, not luck; they then discover the highlights and shortcomings of each subject: their eminence or mediocrity, what could be more and what could be less. There is no place here for emotion or deceit. These two are the celebrated pitfalls of success: to deceive oneself and to

---

71   The Muses and Graces were Greek goddesses of knowledge, intelligence, and talent, while Minerva was the Roman goddess of wisdom. In other words, wise men coming together to confabulate is divine in nature.

be deceived by others. You are always to be an integrated judge of reason, who without eyes sees more and without hands touches and feels all. Great happiness is freedom of judgment, free from the tyranny of ignorance or favoritism; it originates from the center of wisdom, although, perhaps for security or affection, the Complete Man may sometimes want to tuck her (wisdom) inside the citadel of his heart, keeping her a secret and all to himself.

In addition to being a delight, being a man of judgment and observation brings great understanding of objects and of the subjects of things, as well as their causes, effects, and affects. But their greatest enhancement is the most profitable, giving him the ability to discern between the discrete and the foolish, the remarkable and the vulgar. For just as the greatest strategy for cards is knowing which one to keep and which one to discard, the greatest rule for living is to know which people to keep around you for a winning hand.

As an example of this, we can look to the judicious, the knowledgeable, and the master of acumen and acuity, His Excellency the Duke of Híjar[72], who is an oracle of wisdom and understanding and who is personally known to the author, not only in title but in eminent reality. His teachings are echoed in this instruction.

----

72   Jaime Francisco Sarmiento de Silva, 5th Duke of Híjar.

XX

A Man Against Self-Aggrandizement

Satire

Oh, that great teacher, the one who began to teach by unteaching! His first lesson was to ignore what they already knew and help them unlearn all the nonsense they had been taught; unlearning foolishness is no less important than gaining knowledge. Therefore, Antisthenes[73] ordered his subjects to unlearn their frivolity first in order to better learn successes later.

It is a matter of great importance to acquire the unique jewels of virtue, but it is of greater importance to first flee your vulgar defects, because one alone is enough to overshadow them all, and even all together, they are not enough to deny one alone. The smallest mischief or mistake, of but a fraction, is enough to condemn and banish you entirely in the eyes of the secular world, and all the beauty of the virtues you possess will not contain enough absolution to acquit you. God forgives; man does not.

Defects that are blatantly known as such are easily declined by any moderately discreet and sensible person. But there

---

73   Antisthenes was a Greek philosopher and a pupil of Socrates. He adopted and developed the ethical side of Socrates's teachings, advocating an ascetic life lived in accordance with virtue. Later writers regarded him as the founder of Cynic philosophy.

are some so concealed and covered by a thin layer of perfection that they try to pass as enhancements, especially when they have authority.[74]

One of these defects is the exaggeration and display of good fortune and success, which aspires not to embody excellence but to gain esteem and find favor with great personages; it interferes in everything, from correspondence to diplomacy, and even with virtue; it disguises itself, pretending to border on the heroic, but it really does not. It signals to wise men that your mouth and stomach can only afford very little, and they are not accustomed to securing large mouthfuls of fortune.

Those who have the least are very much like a treasure hunter, because they hunt for opportunities and exaggerate their exploits; only when things are worth less than nothing does one feel the need to make them seem more expensive, make others wait to create mystery, or try to astonish with the smallest of things. These chameleons of applause make sure all things seem the best and all actions are exploits; life is all portents, events, miracles of fortune, and affairs of fame. They make certain that there is nothing ordinary about them; they make all things into singularities of courage, knowledge, and happiness, giving everyone a glut of wonderment.

It is foolish to fade into insignificance, but boasting is intolerable. The Complete Man aspires to be great rather than to appear to be so. He is content with who he is and what he has, and thus there is no internal struggle in him to be liked for anything other than reality; and, rather than trying to exaggerate what he has accomplished out of insecurity, in

---

74   Gracián tells us here that there are two types of defects within us: the ones that are blatant and obvious, which any sensible person can see and correct through self-policing, and those that we have concealed and may actually consider assets when they, in fact, are not.

his maturity, he views a little as a lot, and he is grateful for it in silence and solitude.

Exaggerations are born of a faded littleness and a dejected inclination, and this very ridiculousness discredits them. Such men seem incredible, but they are not, and, sadly, so many of them are like this. We bump into them daily and are forced to hear their ridiculous exaggerations, even though we would rather run away from them. Pride always lies, and where it most seeks esteem, it is met with contempt; when it presumes to be admired, it is laughed at by all.

It is not born of a high spirit but of a vileness of heart; it does not aspire to true honor but to apparent honor; not to true feats and achievements but to facades. In this way, there are some who are not soldiers but wish to be and who do everything they can to look the part and try to appear as though they are.

They look for occasions to exploit, and if the slightest opportunity is offered to them, they exaggerate that chance in the name of self-aggrandizement, and if you did not know any better, you would think they were the bellicose and lucky Marquis of Torrecuso[75] in the midst of a breakthrough in the trenches of Fuenterrabía[76] or rescuing Perpignan[77] or, as he did so many times, dismantling the brave and numerous armies of France.

---

75   Gerolamo Maria Caracciolo, Marqués de Torrecuso, was a Spanish aristocrat and soldier born in the Kingdom of Naples in the 17th century. He rose through the ranks of the Spanish army, becoming Governor of Navarre, and served extensively during the Thirty Year War and the Catalan Revolt.

76   Fuenterrabía is a city and municipality in the Basque Country, in northern Spain.

77   Perpignan was besieged and captured by the French during the Thirty-Year War in September 1642.

They present themselves as great ministers, exhibiting zeal and occupation; great men always making business out of nothing. They raise dust from specks and a lot of noise from quiet things; they sell themselves as though they are very busy, hungry for rest and time; they speak of mystery; in each gesture, they portend depths, exclamations, and warnings, and like this, they deceive, with their mechanisms that garner attention but have little depth.

Others go around begging for opportunities that they can use to self-aggrandize themselves, like little ants of honor; the slightest opportunity in which they are allowed to engage inflates their ego, and they turn into chariots of showcasing, telling everyone of their exploit and exaggerating it, of course.

They become very much like chickens, which cluck all day and then lay one egg. They walk with their shoulders back and chests out, like proud and swollen mountains, yet all they did was get rid of a mouse.

There is a great difference between being a master of exploits and an exploiter. Even when faced with true opposition, the former, because of his great eminence, feels no need to affect, embellish, or exaggerate what he engages in; he is content with doing and leaves it to others to tell and speak of his greatness.

If the Great Caesar commented on himself, it was only because his modesty exceeded his courage; he was not exaggerating but speaking the truth. But great men like Caesar are few and far between. Most look for feats and achievements in order to sell them and even make them seem more expensive, inventing traces just to flaunt them in order to get ahead. One success for them, born out of luck, even after a thousand civil and even criminal errors, is enough to embolden them to proclaim it to everyone, and, not finding enough pens to write about their successes, they rent gold pens so that they can write their nonsense under the guise of sanity.

These fools make great feats of their nothingness, and although they use their passion as an excuse, in the end, their foolishness causes everything to come crashing down. Their exaggerations and aggrandizement are so frequent and great that they force others to drink from their cup of nonsense until those they impose upon are quickly fed up with them. Make no mistake about this: the fact that these idolaters of ignorance venerate their folly is an inexcusable, vulgar thing. Politicians too are very much like this, violated by dependency; ignorance and affected praise come out of their teeth because they are flatterers of malice, and, to be honest, whether or not they proceed from deceit is of no consequence, for even if they are absolved of ignorance, they are still condemned to flattery. To be a fool for the cause and benefit of another is to fall into foolishness in one's own home and vanity in that of others.

Domitian's[78] accomplishments were not triumphs but exaggerated exploits; Emperor Caesar and Emperor Augustus, who did have triumphs worthy of boasting, objected to grand-scale adulations, while Caligula and Nero applauded their deeds in an attempt to pass them off as great feats, but they were, in fact, nothing but rubbish. These two would kill a wild boar and try to pass it off as if they had just conquered a country.

----

78   The Roman Emperor Domitian was hated by Rome, largely because of his cruelty and showiness, yet he insisted on being addressed as "master and god." In 96 AD, he was murdered by a group that included praetorian guards, palace officials, and even his own wife.

The feathers of fame are not made of gold, but they resonate more than sonorous silver. They are expensive and give the merits of applause.[79]

---

79   Do not put all your faith in fame. While it is valuable and brings applause, it is not made of gold and, therefore, it is not everlasting.

XXI

A Man of Diligence and Intelligence

Metaphorical

Nature first formed two beings, and evil reduced them to none; then knowledge, industry, and commerce came and blinded that one and shrunk this one, and both were still useless. Then Wisdom arrived, invoked by necessity, and gave them a remedy for alternating relief in reciprocal dependence.[80]

"You, blind man," said Wisdom, "lend your feet to the lame, and you, lame man, lend your eyes to the blind." They listened and were remedied. The blind man then took on his shoulders the one who was lame, and so now the lame had feet and the blind had eyes, and like this they led each other.

----

80   Here, Gracián mentions the creation of Adam and Eve and how their fall reduced them to nothing. Then, when knowledge, industry, and commerce arrived, they separated humans according to their capabilities; some did better than others, but in the end, "both were still useless", alluding to the spiritual and moral bankruptcy of man due to his sin and iniquity.

Gracián then tells us that wisdom arrived, heavenly sent, and changed man's one-way trajectory towards darkness—a reference to Christ.

He then moves to explain the importance of mastering the art of wisdom, for it is of "reciprocal dependence," meaning that wisdom uses man to teach itself to others, and man uses wisdom as a way to alleviate his wretchedness.

He further illustrates this in the ensuing paragraph.

The latter called the former his light, and the former called the latter his heaven.

A wise man saw them working together and, coveting the chance to make wisdom his own ingenious emblem, asked, "Well, how did you figure this out? Who was first to act? Did the blind lead the lame, or did the lame lead the blind?" And they answered in this way:

> "One needs diligence as much as he needs intelligence. One without the other is worth little, but together they can accomplish a lot. The former quickly executes what the latter stopped and meditated on. Together, diligence and intelligence execute and crown with success well-intentioned attention."

> "We once saw a very diligent man working on great things; he was an executive and very efficient but not at all intelligent, and a wise man passed him by as others were praising his diligence and said to himself, 'If he were as intelligent as he is diligent, he would undoubtedly be a great minister to a great monarch.'"

And still, you cannot fully trust those who are diligent alone, because great risk lies in their diligence; they err quickly if they are left alone, and they use all of their efficiency rather than their intelligence to fix their errors. And so it is not a matter of ending things but of ending things with them—those who seem to run like wild horses from post to post—so as to never fall for their foolishness.

It is a good thing that these men commonly abhor advice and exchange it for execution; this makes them easy to spot and easy to avoid.

It is a passion of fools to be very diligent because, since they do not know when to stop, they can act carelessly and without qualms; they are always doing, running, and rushing because they do not reason. And because they lack pause, you cannot detect any warning signs, and, even worse, they never warn that they have no warning signs. I suppose that if forced to be with them, it would be better to be blind, because whoever does not have eyes that see will not have to see them.

There are individuals who are good for errands because they execute with the most happy diligence, but who are not worthy of command because they think poorly and choose unwisely, always stumbling into the wrong. There are men of all geniuses, but not everyone can be the first; some men are destined to be second, third, fourth, etc. Be careful that you do not become unfortunate by elevating the unworthy to positions that are undeserved.

But the unhappiness of great intelligence without execution is no less; its conceived successes wither like a flower because, in the ice of hesitancy, it loses its fragrant hope and is spoiled by abandonment.

Some resolve with extreme synderesis[81] and reason, decree with plausible choices, and then lose themselves in execution, spoiling the excellence of their opinions with the ineffectiveness of their actions; they start well and end badly because they stopped; they make a judgment and an appreciation of what is appropriate, and then, due to the fatigue of executing it, they let everything go to waste.

----

81   *Synderesis*, or more correctly, *synteresis*, is a term used by scholastic theologians to signify the habitual knowledge of the universal principles of moral action.

Some are barely applied to what matters most, while others are passionate about what matters least, and both end up developing an antipathy towards their obligations. For these reasons, genius and application do not always fit together, and the difficulty that they encounter in what they undertake when the nature of their talent is misaligned with that of their undertaking, causes them to flee from that undertaking—more from horror than from fear, more from anger than from work. It is a gift, and a great one, to have the opportunity to marry talent with application. Because, most times, one is not given this chance, whether with office, with position, or even with what is sovereign. How often does a man degenerate from the heroic and destined to a very vulgar nothingness because of this.

It is good that wise men are restrained, for it is out of much contemplation that improvement is born. Those who are diligent but lack intelligence not only discover all inconveniences but also prevent all the remedies; diligence can rarely best intelligence. One is desired in those who govern, and the other in those who fight, and in the man where both of these concur, they form a prodigy.

It was the alacrity of Alexander the Great that made him the father of great ventures; he conquered everything by saying to himself, "Leave nothing for tomorrow." Julius Caesar, another great exemplar of heroes, said that his incredible undertakings had been completed before he even consulted his advisers regarding them; their very greatness did not frighten him, and not even thinking about their risks was enough to stop him; his great words were always *"let us go"* and never *"let the others go."* Alacrity, willingness, and keenness—these traits are enough to make the lion, king of the wild beasts; and, although many other beasts are capable of beating him, some in arms, others in body, and others still in strength, he conquers them all with the faith of his readiness.

This is the polarity that the courageous Spaniards and the bellicose Frenchmen maintain between themselves, which equalizes competition and balances Spanish prudence with French readiness. The restraint of the former angers the latter, but what the Spaniards lack in promptness they make up for with their advance, and, for their part, the temerity of the French is a drag on the former's incredible forward progress. Caesar took the pulse of both nations and defeated one by preventing their invasion and the other by waiting.[82] And we cannot forget the Great Emperor Augustus, who, with his *Festina-lente*[83] in company, made for a very successful medium.

Many contradict what is good because it is rare and they cannot understand it, while what is evil has many helpers. The path of truth and success is unique and difficult, for perdition has many means and very few remedies. That which is contrary to our desired outcome usually ends up being the result when we seek that which is convenient; all things get conjured up, and circumstances get blurred. Occasions pass, time runs away, places go missing, the seasons waste away, and all while you're still having breakfast and don't even notice; but intelligence and diligence conquer everything.

----

82   Julius Caesar, as governor of Gaul, prevented a Roman invasion by crossing the Rubicon River and declaring war on Rome before Rome could declare war on him. The second example is a reference to the Battle of Bibracte during the Gallic Wars, wherein the emperor was greatly outnumbered by the Helvetti and, due to his many wounded soldiers, had to wait three days before being able to engage and defeat them.

83   *Festina-lente* is a classic adage meaning "make haste slowly." It implies that activities should be performed with a proper balance of intelligence and diligence. If tasks are rushed too quickly, then problems catch us by surprise, mistakes are made, and good long-term results are not achieved. Gracián suggests that this method of doing things allows one to have foresight as he makes progress, and, gives him the ability to see potential pitfalls so he can ensure success.

-XXII-

A Man of Good Manners

A letter to Dr. Bartolomé de Morlanes, Chaplain of the King and Our Lord, in the Holy Church of Nuestra Señora del Pilar, in Zaragoza, Spain.

By this great precept, my lord, Cleobulus[84] deserved to be the first of the seven sages, and therefore, it is the first and most important of all the precepts. If teaching it was enough to give him a reputation as a sage, imagine then what becomes of those who observe it! Knowing things but not doing them is not being a philosopher but a grammarian.

Both circumstance and substance are required in life; the first thing we come across in people is not their essence but their appearance; from the outside, we come to know their inside, and by their behavior, we judge their bearing. In other words, we judge those we do not know by their comportment.

Good manners are one of the jewels of merit, and they can be acquired; for this reason, the lack of them is inexcusable. While in some it is born of their naturalness and helped along by ingenuity, in others it is entirely a creation of art. Art can remedy the forgetfulness of nature and even improve

----

84   Cleobulus of Lindos, also known as "Cleobulus the Wise," was one of the Seven Sages of Greece.

it. What is even better is when nature and art come together to form a pleasant man, equal in both ease and happiness.

It is also one of the transcendental beauties that affect all action and employment. Strong is the truth, brave is reason, and powerful is justice, but without good manners, they fade rather than shine, and with them, everything moves forward. Good manners make up for any fault, even ones of reason, gilding with gold the iron of error, applying makeup to the faces of ugliness, denying slights, and concealing everything that is abhorrent.

How many serious and important matters have been spoiled by bad manners, and how many of those already evicted were rescued and improved by good!

The great zeal of a minister, the courage of a leader, the knowledge of a scholar, and the power of a prince are not enough if this very important formality does not accompany them all.

It is the political adornment of scepters, the jewel of crowns, and in no other job is it more important and urgent than in command, where it forces others to feel obliged, for superiors win more hearts through humanity than despotism.

Seeing a king lay aside his superiority to show his humanness and courtesy forces his subjects to bend their knee and feel doubly indebted to him; it is first necessary to reign in people's hearts in order to later govern their will. It reconciles the grace of the people and then garners their applause, if not by nature, then by art. Those who admire good manners, good comportment, and warmth in an individual do not look at whether it is naturally born of him or whether it is an art cultivated by him over time; either way, he is greeted with acclaim.

There are things that are esteemed more for their manner than their being. A clever manner can arouse nostalgia for the past, bring it back, and make it seem as if it were new again. If circumstances are perfected, they deny the tiredness of the old. Good taste always goes forward, never goes backward, does not focus on what has already happened, and always bites into novelty. A fresh set of circumstances can freshen up what is stale and often repeated, which is usually intolerable and even more so in imitations, which can never reach either the sublimity or the novelty of that which came first.

This is also true in matters of wit and wisdom, as even when things are well known, they are made more palatable if they are spoken of with a different rhetoric or written by the historian in a fresh literary style.

When things are exquisite and perfected, you can never tire anyone by repeating them, not even if they are repeated six or seven times. But although they do not tire, they also do not cause any new admiration, and so it is necessary to bake them in a different way so that they cause a new aroma. New novelties are always flattering; their new taste always enchants, and by seasoning old foods with new herbs, you renew interest in them; this is the secret to longevity.

How many very vulgar and ordinary things have been enhanced and turned into something new and excellent, and then sold to those with the highest taste and admiration for the exquisite! And, on the contrary, how many choice things lacking this spice have been cast into the seas of indifference and forgotten?

The man of good manners takes pride in his discretion. The same words that can flatter one man can offend another, so what matters is not what you say but how you say it. There can be so much difference and therefore importance in the how; if a lack of grace at any moment can condemn a good man, how much more will it affect the man who is deliberately unpleasant and, even more so, those men in positions of command? Affectations, arrogance, dryness, rudeness, insufferableness, and other parallel monstrosities make a man unapproachable.

"It is a little mischief," a wise man pondered, "yet the eyebrow one constantly raises is enough to upset his entire life."[85] And, conversely, the pleasantness of a warm countenance promises the pleasantness of a warm spirit, its beauty strengthening the softness within.

Above all, pride yourself on gilding your "no," so that it will be valued more than a reluctant "yes." Learn to sweeten truths with such skill that they pass for flattery, and learn to turn unpleasant truths into compliments, telling people not what they are but what they could be.

Perfecting this art creates a refuge for those whom nature forgot and who therefore lack it naturally and who, with it, help themselves achieve more with good manners and a warm disposition than others with their innate talent. It reinforces a man by supplying him with what he essentially lacks and, with the advantages it affords him, makes him superior to the natural. And its greatest advantage is that it will always remain a mystery to those it flatters because it cannot be defined since what it consists of is unknown. So

----

85   **An eyebrow raised is seen as a sign of disapproval and anger. Here Gracián reminds us of a wise man's advice: do not go through life constantly angry and with a bad temper, or you will ruin it entirely.**

let us just say that they are the Three Graces, together forming a composite of all perfection.

And because we do not always appeal to antiquity for prodigies or beg for the heroic of the past, we should focus our admiration and applause on the present by looking for this jewel in the Catholic, in the heroic, in the great Queen, Our Lady Doña Isabel de Borbón[86], the one who not only continued but advanced the glory of the renowned successes of the Great Catholic Queens of Spain. Among her many remarkable crowned exaltations, she superimposed herself in the hearts of her subjects and was such a pleasing sovereign that she stole the hearts of her vassals and bewitched their affections, collecting all of humanity with a warmth that mirrored the divine. She did a lot in a short time, lived plausibly, and died in tears. Evil envied her and, together with death, rose up to take her from this world.

But the sovereignty of God is an unstoppable force that always has its way, and instead of giving evil the chance to claim her, the Holy One welcomed her into heaven as both an angel and a saint. She was sent to us so that she could improve our condition and happiness, and once she did, God snatched her away and gave her eternal glory and everlasting peace.

----

86   Isabel de Borbón, also known as Elisabeth of France, was Queen of Spain from 1602 to 1644 and was renowned for her beauty, intelligence, noble personality, and diplomacy. She died at the very young age of 41 from an unknown illness.

-XXIII-

The Art of Being Fortunate

A Fable

Fortune is always in disguise; many complain about her, few feel gratitude toward her, and this discontent reaches even the wild beasts! But fortune is also a great revelator: those who are seen complaining of her the loudest are the most simple-minded.

There was once a simple donkey who went through life complaining about his fortune. He went from group to group and found not only compassion but also applause, especially from the vulgar and the dullards.

Then one day, advised by many but accompanied by none, this simple donkey went to appear at the general assembly of the sovereign creator, Almighty God. Here, deeply humbled (something that is always welcomed in fools), he kneeled before the golden throne of God, asked for permission to be heard, and delivered this horrendous tirade:

"Oh, Almighty God, I wish you to be righteous and not vengeful; here you have before your majestic presence the most unhappy and ignorant of wild brutes. And I am requesting not so much vengeance against the wrongs that have been done to me but rather a remedy for my misfortunes. How does it happen, O Eternal God, that you allow your sovereignty to be distributed by Fortune, who is blind towards me, is a tyrant, and is an evil stepmother? Why does she ignore me and sometimes torment me? I'm just a simple beast! Why does this cruel lady burden me and add to my unhappiness with the surcharges of misfortune? She makes me both confused and discontent; she persecutes my innocence and favors malice; the proud lion triumphs; the cruel tiger lives; the sly fox, who deceives everyone, laughs at everyone; and the voracious wolf is never held accountable. I alone, who does the least to anyone, am harmed by all. I eat little, work the most, and still you allow her to treat me with a short carrot and a long stick. I always look unkempt and ugly, even to myself, and cannot go out among people. And the worst indignity of all this is having to pull the carts of ungrateful peasants from one place to another."

This pitiful proclamation greatly moved everyone in the assembly except the Almighty, who, seeing both the forests and the trees, is not so vulgarly persuaded. Then Almighty God put a finger on his lips, signaling to the assembly that he wanted their silence. He then said, "My dear donkey, your complaints seem valid, but I would like to hear Fortune's side of the story!" He then turned to the archangels Raphael[87] and Uriel[88] and said, "Bring Fortune to me; I would like to speak with her publicly."

The most senior archangels assembled a legion of angels and hurried off to find her. They searched many parts of the world and found her nowhere. Not wanting to let down their creator, they planned and strategized but, in the end, had no answers as to where she might be or how to find

---

87   Raphael is charged with healing people and animals from any number of difficulties, both mental and physical.

88   Uriel is the angel of wisdom. He is charged with providing aid in intellectual pursuits, particularly problem-solving, by shining the light of God's truth into darkness and confusion.

her. They went back to heaven and entered the house of the mighty command, where the rest of the archangels were. By that time, the severity of the problem had already reached their ears, and they too were deeply concerned.

They came together and, after much deliberation, concluded that, first and foremost and without a doubt, Fortune had little or nothing to do with their confusion and restlessness. They then decided to set out and personally speak to Wealth and Wisdom. Wealth had doubtlessly seen her most recently, so they decided to knock on his door first. When they did, Worry answered. It explained that Fortune had been there, taken everything, and left. And so on they went to speak with Wisdom. On their way to Wisdom's house, they ran into Foolishness, who, like a fool, asked no questions. When they arrived, they knocked, and Poverty answered the door. It explained that Fortune was not there either but was expected any day.[89]

As the ministers of the Sovereign God left Wisdom's house, they noticed another house standing alone at the end of a very narrow path. They knocked and knocked until finally a beautiful maiden came and answered the door. Marveled by her beauty, the archangels asked her for her name, and she responded, "My name is Virtue."

As they spoke, Fortune emerged from deep in the house; she was smiling. The ministers served her with the Almighty's subpoena, and she immediately obeyed, flying off to present herself before his throne.

----

89   Poverty answered the door at Wisdom's house and said, "Fortune is expected any day." Meaning that wisdom is found in poverty; in the valleys of life, not on the mountain peaks. But once found, Fortune quickly follows.

She came very reverently to kneel before the sacred throne, and as she approached it, everyone in the assembly bowed and curtsied. The All-Powerful Deity smiled warmly at her and said: "What are all these complaints about you that I am constantly hearing, Fortune? Every single day, I get complaints about your behavior. Today in particular, I have this poor donkey before me with some very serious and seemingly true accusations against you. My dearest Fortune, I am not upset with you. I understand better than anyone how difficult it is to please most people and how impossible it is to please all people. Most people are not grateful for the abundance that they have and instead complain about the little that they lack. When they look at someone else, they see only his good luck and none of his misfortune. They see the jewels in his crown, but not its weight or worry. Therefore, I pay little to no attention to their whining; but I must say, the complaints of this poor, simple donkey seem valid. What do you have to say for yourself?" Fortune looked at the donkey out of the corner of her eye; she was about to smile but, remembering where she was, collected herself, regained her composure, and very simply said: Almighty God, Supreme Ruler of All, I want a simple sentence to discharge and acquit me of these charges, and it is this:

"He is more of an ass than a donkey!"

The entire assembly of God burst into laughter upon hearing this, and even the Supreme Deity began to laugh. Then, rather than console the donkey, God moved to instruct and teach him: "Unhappy brute, you would not be so unhappy if you behaved more wisely and acted a little sharper. Rather than complain about others, you should learn from them. Learn to be as alert as the lion, as prudent as the elephant, as determined as the tiger, as clever as the fox, and as crafty as the wolf. Make a plan as to how you will achieve this; wisely execute those plans, and you will succeed in your attempts; and, eventually, you will stop being so unfortunate."

Then Almighty God then stood up, raised his voice, and said: "All of you mortals, do not be deceived; the only luck and the only misfortune that exist are wisdom and folly in your personal choices."

-XXIV -

The Crown of Discretion

Tribute

God once called Wisdom into his presence and charged it with the task of putting in order the jewels that adorn the immortal crown of discretion. And so Wisdom flew to earth and found itself a man; it then began to explain to him how much stronger his mind and body would be if his tongue were weakened and kept under control. A contest ensued as his tongue immediately began to speak, not allowing him to ponder the significance of this instruction; and, unable to stop his own tongue, he confirmed that Wisdom did not exaggerate when it spoke of the tongue's vulgar efforts and destruction.

The tongue, never lacking, continued to defend itself by blaming the heart, which, being the principle of life and the king of the other members, is the essence of the flesh. Then he blamed the brain, which, being the seat of synderesis[90] and reason, knows all, but it was of no use to the tongue because both the heart and mind defended themselves, the heart asserting its value in providing the body with life and the brain articulating how it gives man morality through understanding and reason.

----
90 *Synderesis*, **or more correctly,** *synteresis*, **is a term used by scholastic theologians to signify the habitual knowledge of the universal principles of moral action.**

The tongue, feeling pressed and knowing that the mind and heart are strongest when it is weakest, said, "Do I seem so weak to you? I am stronger than all of you, able to speak of the most complex anomalies, and able to break the strongest of wills."

Everyone burst out laughing, as they usually do, especially the teeth, who always make a pretense of stopping him. Then Wisdom interjected and said, "The only power you have, tongue, is the ability to speak the truth. But without the heart to give you proper timing so as not to offend, and without the mind to give you the ability to speak that which he has already reasoned to be true, you are weak, can harm a man's entire being, and easily lacerate others with your weakness. Without the heart, you are cruel, and without the mind, you can only speak of stupidities."

Wisdom continued: "And without the mind, the heart drowns in a sea of emotions. Therefore, strong is the king who finishes everything; stronger is the woman who collects everything; strong is the wine, which drowns reason; but strongest is the man who calms the emotional seas of his heart with reason and orders his tongue to speak only when there is something intelligent to say."

"True, true," they all exclaimed and gave up.

Thus it happened in that famous contest between the sublime jewels that adorn the golden crown of the perfect man, a contest that they had among themselves that was decided by Wisdom on God's golden globe. Upon hearing this, the divine then decreed that the mind, the heart, and the tongue, in that order, form the apex of this immortal crown of discretion.

Within this crown there are highness of mind, majesty of spirit, authority, esteem, reputation, universality, ostentation, gallantry, cleanliness, plausibility, good taste, culture, grace, lordship, patience, sympathy, incomprehensibility, indispensability, sharpness, good manners, retentiveness, knowledge, the judicious, the unpassionate, the unaffected, the serious, the practical, the executive, the attentive, and many others that add to this crown of grandeur.

You first see this crown adorning the heads of those great men of antiquity, whose spirits come to rest among those who are worthy of them only after their careful study. These were, although few, the greatest men of the centuries, giants of fame and prodigies of eminence who, in the end, all became immortal heroes.

Later, you see this crown shining in the lives of passionate, diligent, and powerful men; each one advancing with the help of his particular talent and gift of enhancement; the wise by reason, the brave by force, and the powerful by authority; each one with such tenacity of immortality and with such an inflammation of courage that the whole realm of heroism would burn if they were ever to go to war with each other.

Fame's run varies, and fortune is equivocal, contingent on the times, their uses, and the geniuses of the people; when one's feelings abound, victory can never be declared. Wise men consider chaos to be the child of confusion, and they deal with this child through reason, not emotion. They rely first on the mind, then the heart, and finally the tongue in order to bring it to heel.

And now, what do we make of Astrea[91], who abandoned the world and retired to heaven at a time when it was just for Momus[92] to curse everyone—when wickedness, greed, gossip, and corruption had strangled justice and condemned everything? Truth remained, but it had been wounded for so long that it retreated to its interior, pretended to have a cold, and even became mute. Zeus subsequently transformed her into the constellation of Virgo and sent her to live among the stars; she took his thunderbolt with her to one day return and implement justice. But I say she already dwells among us, in the form of the one virtue that enhances the brilliance of the jewels that adorn the golden crown of the Complete Man.

God was sitting in his court in the noon-light when the mind, the heart, and the tongue were commenting to each other on what had been said about them, and they began to commend one another for the way in which they had been referred to. The Almighty praised them all, each for their own uniqueness, but at the end he declared his thoughts, saying:

"Most eminent jewels of the cultured and discreet man, I confess as your Creator that I admire you all and celebrate

----

91   In Greek mythology, Astrea was the personification of justice. She was the daughter of Zeus and was usually found sitting next to him, carrying his thunderbolt, a symbol that she was the administrator of his justice. She left the world of mortals out of disgust at the corruption and wickedness that had spread among humanity. The ancient Greeks believed that one day she would return to earth, administer justice, and mark the beginning of a new golden age.

92   Momus was the god of mockery, blame, ridicule, scorn, complaint, and harsh criticism. He was expelled by Zeus from heaven for ridiculing the gods; he is generally considered evil. Here, Gracián says that when man is wicked, he invites the blame, criticism, and condemnation of evil upon himself. A master of theology, Gracián undoubtedly creates this concept from the bible passages that point to Satan as the accuser of man before a sovereign and just God. See Job 2, Zechariah 3:1-2, and Revelation 12:10.

you all, but I cannot help but tell the truth; I say then that your brilliance can only shine off the reflection of this one virtue, from the splendor of its heroism and its complementary discretion. It is hated by many but respected by all; Seneca called it *the only good of man;* Aristotle, *his perfection;* Sallust, *immortal blazon;* Cicero, *the cause of happiness;* Apuleyo, *likeness of the divine;* Sophocles, *perpetual and constant wealth;* Euripides, *a hidden coin;* Socrates, *a cause for fortune;* Virgilio, *beauty of the soul;* Cato, *the foundation of authority.* By itself, it is a diamond! Isocrates possessed it; Menander had it as his shield; and Horacio had it as his best quiver. Valerio Máximo found it invaluable; Plautus considered it his greatest prize; and the Great Caesar called it the beginning and end; and I, the Almighty Creator, call it, in a word, *Integrity.*"[93]

----
93   Here, Gracián subtly gives a list of men he considers worthy of studying and emulating.

-XXV-

A Man of Wise Distribution

The Complete Man lives out his life as though he were going to live for both a short and a long amount of time. Life without rest is like a long journey without an inn. For what if you get to spend time in the company of Heraclitus![94] God, in his wisdom, has ordered nature to proportion the life of man according to the path of the sun and the four ages of man to the four seasons of the year.[95]

Spring begins in joyful childhood, with its tender flowers and fragile hopes. Followed by the hot and temperate summer of youth, dangerous in any case because of the burning of the blood and stormy passions. Then enters the desired autumn of the age of man, crowned with fruits that are seasoned in opinions, wisdom, knowledge, and successes.

Then it all ends in the frozen winter of old age: the leaves of the valor fall to the floor, white hair appears like snow, the streams of the veins are frozen, teeth and hair disappear, and

----

94   Here, Gracián instructs one to always be well rested, because if fortune favors you and you find yourself in the company of a wise man, you want to be alert and with a fresh mind so that you can maximize the opportunity and learn from him.

95   "proportion the life of man according to the path of the sun." A man gets older every year, and every year the earth completes one entire rotation around the sun.

life begins to shiver and tremble in the presence of death. In this way, nature creates a parallel between the seasons and age.

Art, which rivals nature, tries to distribute virtue over time in a similar manner, giving the genius a choice. Pythagoras[96] said it with a single letter, and in its two branches, he encrypted the two very opposite paths of evil and good. They say that Hercules arrived at dawn and that he was perplexed. He looked at the path to the left with fondness and the one on the right with horror. The latter was narrow and difficult, uphill, and less traveled. The former was spacious and easy, downhill, and often traveled. He stopped and noticed a superior hand guiding him impulsively down the path of virtue on the right, to the whereabouts of heroism.[97]

He who spoke gracefully and sang sweetly, the great Falco[98], whose singing turned him into a swan, said that God gave man thirty years to rejoice and enjoy himself; then twenty years were borrowed from the donkey to work; another twenty from the dog, in which to bark; and another twenty from the monkey, in which to grow old and die. A most excellent fable, full of truths.

There was once a man who divided comedy into three acts and the voyage of his life into three seasons. In the first season, he used to talk to the dead; in the second, to the living;

----

96   Pythagoras was a Greek philosopher well known in ancient times for the mathematical achievement of the Pythagorean theorem. Gracián is referencing the letter "Y" in this text. Using conceptism, he likens the letter to arriving at a critical crossroad in life.

97   Gracián is referring to a story called "Hercules at the Crossroads." It concerns the young Hercules, who is offered a choice between vice and virtue—a life of pleasure or one of hardship and honor. In the early modern period, it became a popular motif in Western art. The meaning here is that as we get older, life gives us wisdom and virtue and then moves to test our faithfulness to them.

98   Jaume Joan Falco, Valencian poet and mathematician.

and in the third, to himself. Now, come, let us decipher the little riddle.

I say that the first third of his life was devoted to books and reading, which was more of an enjoyment than work; one is more of a man the more he knows, and so learning should be his first occupation; he devoured books, which are food for the soul and delights for the spirit. What great happiness to learn from these masters and their mastered subjects! He learned all the arts worthy of the noble mind and the ingenious, as opposed to those arts that felt more like enslavement and work. He prepared himself with great effort to arm himself with a cognition of languages: the two universal languages, English and Spanish, which today are the keys to the world; and the singular Greek, Italian, French, and German, in order to achieve greatness through the good that has become eternal in them.

Then he gave himself to the great mother of life, the wife of understanding, and the daughter of experience—laudable history, the great elucidator of life, and the art that teaches and most instructs. He began with antiquity and arrived at modernity, although some do the opposite. He spared neither his own nor foreign histories, neither those that are sacred nor the profane. With choice and careful estimation, he chose the authors, carefully distinguishing times, eras, and centuries; undertaking great understandings of monarchies, republics, and empires, with their increases, declines, and changes; the number, order, and qualities of their princes; and their deeds in peace and in war. And all of this with such a fine memory that his mind became a spacious theater for all of antiquity.

He walked through the delightful gardens of poetry, not so much to use it as to enjoy it, which is an advantage and makes one decent. After all that, he was neither so ignorant that he did not know how to write one poem nor was he so inconsiderate as to write two. He read all the true poets, greatly advancing his cleverness with their maxims and sharpening his judgment with their wisdom, and, together with those tools, he dedicated the bulk of his time to the profound Horacio[99] and the penetrating Martial[100], committing them to memory and understanding. He joined poetry to humanity and letters, creating a treasure of erudition.

He went on to the beautiful gardens of philosophy and to the very beginning of nature, reaching the causes of things, the composition of the universe, the artificial being of man, the properties of animals, the virtues of herbs, and the qualities of precious stones. He found the most enjoyment in moral philosophy, in the nourishment of those who are truly wise, and in giving life to wisdom. He pursued the wisdom of the sages and of the philosophers, who bequeathed it to us in their adages, aphorisms, emblems, and fables. He was a great disciple of Seneca, an impassioned student of Plato, of the Seven Sages of Greece, of Epictetus, Plutarch, and of the useful and gracious Aesop.

He learned cosmography, both its physics and math, measuring the lands and the seas, distinguishing the places and climates, the four parts of the universe[101], the provinces and nations, the kingdoms and republics, sometimes only to know of them and others to speak about them, in order to not be counted among the ignorant and vulgar, whose laziness keeps them from ever knowing where their feet are resting. From astrology, he learned as much as sanity allowed.

----

99   Quintus Horatius Flaccus, known as Horace in English, was the leading Roman poet during the time of Augustus.

100   Martial has been called the greatest Latin epigrammatist and is considered the creator of the modern epigram.

101   The four parts of the universe: Space, Time, Matter, and Energy.

He recognized the celestial bodies, noted their various movements, numbered their stars and planets, and observed their influences and effects.

He crowned his practical studiousness with the most profitable of all readings: a continuous and serious study of the Sacred Scriptures, which delighted the phoenix of kings, Don Alfonso the Magnanimous[102], who, in the midst of so many and such heroic feats, scrutinized the Bible from cover to cover fourteen times with comment.

With this, he achieved a knowledgeable universality, so that his moral philosophy made him prudent, natural, and wise. With history, he was made cautious, and with poetry, he was made ingenious. With rhetoric, he became eloquent, and with humanity, he became discreet.

Cosmography made him well informed, and the sacred scriptures made him pious and reverent; and all of this together made him consummate, a man who could compete with His Excellency Don Sebastian de Mendoza, 5th Count of Coruña. This first season is the great and first act of life.

He spent the second season of his life in pleasant travels, where he found constant elation in curiosity and observation. He sought and enjoyed all the good and the best in the world, for whoever does not see things tangibly cannot fully enjoy them, and those who see things only once enjoy them more than those who see them often, because the former rejoices and the latter annoys. Taste is always preserved for those first fruits that have not been eaten continuously,

----

102   Alfonso V, also known as Alfonso the Magnanimous, was King of Aragon and Naples; he is considered one of Europe's most brilliant monarchs.

for the first of a new thing delights only its owner; after that, only others can be delighted.

His travels allowed him to communicate with the greatest men in the world, eminent either in letters, in valor, or in the arts, all esteeming eminence, and all this with a judicious understanding, noting, examining, collating, and giving to each thing its deserved appreciation.

Thus he traversed the entire universe and toured all of its political provinces: rich Spain, populous France, beautiful England, crafty Germany, courageous Poland, pleasant Moscovia, and Italy, where all of the aforementioned come together. He admired its most famous emporiums, requesting in each city everything remarkable, both ancient and modern: the magnificence of its temples, the sumptuousness of its buildings, the correctness of its government, the understanding of its citizens, the splendor of its nobility, and all while learning from its scholars and their refined behavior.

He frequented the courts of the greatest princes, admiring in them all the wonders of nature and art in paintings, statues, tapestries, bookstores, jewelry, weapons, gardens, and museums.

He communicated with the first and greatest men in the world, eminent in court, courage, and the arts, while esteeming any sign of excellence, and all this with a judicious understanding, noting, censoring, comparing, and giving each its deserved appreciation.

The third season of such a beautiful life is the biggest and the best, and he spends it meditating on all he has read and all he has seen. Everything that enters through the doors of his senses, the emporium of his soul, he filters through understanding; everything is recorded in his mind. He ponders, judges, discusses, infers, and extracts the meaning of all things with a sixth sense. He digests all his readings first, then devours all he has seen, then later meditates on everything he has read and seen, allowing it to ruminate in his mind; he reduces complex issues by breaking them down, unravels things, discovers truths, and, like this, he feeds the spirit of true wisdom that now resides inside of him.

Old age is destined for contemplation, as the soul gains strength and the body loses it; the superior part of us grows stronger while the inferior part decays. Maturity brings perspective and a different concept of things, and with that maturity, intellect and emotions are seasoned.

A prudent and philosophical reflection on things is very important; it allows us to see fully what we only glimpsed and misunderstood in our youth. Seeing makes one knowledgeable, but contemplating makes one wise.

All those ancient philosophers traveled and made pilgrimages, first gaining knowledge by exploring with their eyes and later gaining wisdom by contemplating with their intelligence what they had seen; this is why they were so rare. The crown of wisdom is knowing how to philosophize and draw from everything like a solicitous bee: either honey, with its usefulness and fine taste, or wax, for the candles of disappointment.

Philosophy is nothing other than meditating on death; we must meditate on it often in order to die well once.[103]

----
103   Here, Gracián is referring to Seneca's famous statement: "You will live poorly if you do not learn how to die well." Death visits us constantly, but through philosophy, we can deal with it effectively and not cause ourselves more suffering than is necessary.

Works by Baltasar Gracián

El Héroe (1637)

El Político (1640)

El Arte de Ingenio (1642)

El Discreto (1646)

El Oráculo Manual y Arte de Prudencia (1647)

El Criticón (1651–1657)

El Comulgatorio (1655)

About the Translator

Website: https://StVitus.Dance
Email: TheMikeSanPedro@gmail.com

9 781945 028525